CLASSIC
EXPERIMENTS
IN MODERN
COLLEGE
CHEMISTRY
I

SECOND EDITION

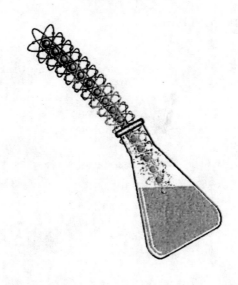

DOUGLAS S. CODY

CHARLES G. HICKS

LEONARD M. ITZKOWITZ

Nassau Community College

Whittier
Publications, Inc.

Published by Whittier Publications, Inc.

Island Park, NY 11561

ISBN   978-1-57604-336-3

Printed in the United States of America

1 0 9 8 7 6 5 4 3 2

TABLE OF CONTENTS

Preface   *iv*

Working with Chemicals   *vii*

Equipment   *viii*

Experiments

    1.   Introduction to the Bunsen Burner and Making Measurements   1

    2.   Mass, Volume and Density   15

    3.   Introduction to Physical Properties   27

    4.   Separation of a Sand-Salt Mixture   41

    5.   Data Collection and Graphing   51

    6.   Paper Chromatography   67

    7.   Boyle's Law   81

    8.   Percent of Potassium Chlorate in a Mixture   91

    9.   Empirical Formula of a Chloride of Magnesium   101

    10.   Molecular Mass of a Volatile Liquid   111

    11.   Calorimetry and Specific Heat   121

    12.   Conductivity, Bonding and Ionic Reactions   131

    13.   Building Molecular Models from Lewis Structures   145

    14.   Water of Hydration   167

Appendices

    A.   Reading a Volumetric Device   A-1

    B.   Conversion Factors   A-2

PREFACE

To the Student

All progress in science is based upon experimentation. While the development of theories may spur the design of new experiments, no theory can gain the acceptance of the scientific community without experimental data that supports it. While each generation of scientists seeks to further extend scientific understanding, they must also understand the conclusions of the accepted science upon which they build.

Although the experiments that you will perform have been done before, keep in mind that, *for you*, they are original research. *For you*, they can lead to new discoveries which should enable you to better understand the material presented in lecture. The experiments included in this manual were chosen because they represent the topics studied, and employ the techniques most often needed for chemical research.

Make every attempt to follow the instructions carefully. If a procedure is lengthy, a way to avoid losing your place and keeping track of the steps done is to put a checkmark in the margin of the procedure as each step is completed. Remember also that your instructor will have suggestions as to procedure and safety. The instructor will tell you if there have been any changes made to the procedure, and the instructor is responsible for safety suggestions in the laboratory. *You, however, have the final responsibility for performing the experiment as correctly and safely as possible.*

In each experiment a purpose is stated and there is an introduction that provides background information about the experiment. All experiments have pre-laboratory assignments that are designed to test your understanding of the introduction. Be sure to read the introduction, as well as the experimental procedure, and complete the pre-laboratory assignment before coming to the laboratory. Be there on time, so that you will hear the pre-laboratory discussion from your instructor. The post-laboratory questions given at the end of the experiment have been designed to summarize the results of the experiment, draw conclusions from the experiment, or reinforce the material relevant to the experiment.

We hope you find the second edition easy to follow and that it makes your experience in the chemistry laboratory a positive, rewarding one.

Notice to the Users

All chemicals present some degree of danger. Therefore it is of utmost importance that they are handled properly and with respect. The authors have made every reasonable attempt to provide appropriate directions, instructions, and safety suggestions for each experiment. The ultimate responsibility for safety however remains with the student and his or her instructor.

Acknowledgements

We would like to thank our colleagues in the chemistry department at Nassau Community College that have provided their professional advice and support. We thank our families for their encouragement and support during preparation of this manual.

We invite the users of this manual to submit corrections and suggestions for improvements.

Douglas S. Cody
Charles G. Hicks
Leonard M. Itkowitz

HANDLING CHEMICALS

1. Solid chemicals are always to be placed in some other container (beaker, weighing boat, weighing paper) when weighed on a balance. They are never place directly on the pan of the balance.

2. Always check the label on any reagent you are going to use. Chemical formulas for different substances may be similar, but not the same. H_2O is water; H_2O_2 is hydrogen peroxide. NaCl is sodium chloride, ordinary table salt; NaCN is sodium cyanide, a deadly poison.

3. Take only the amount of a reagent that you will need for an experiment. Taking too much excess chemical is a waste. This causes unnecessary expense and increases waste disposal problems. Do not, however, *ever* return unused chemicals to their containers, discard them instead.

4. When pouring liquids from a container remove the stopper, keeping the glass stopper between the forefinger and middle finger. Do not put the stopper down on the tabletop, as this may cause contamination of the reagent or damage to the table.

5. Do not touch chemicals with your hands. Never taste chemicals.

6. When diluting acids, always add the acid to the water, rather than in reverse. The dilution of a concentrated acid generates heat which will be dissipated as the acid diffuses down through the water.

HEATING CHEMICALS

1. Adjust the burner so that it gives the proper amount of heat.

2. Never heat a substance in a tightly closed container. Pressure will increase which may cause the top to be ejected or the container to burst.

3. Never look down into the container as you heat it.

4. Be sure the mouth of a test tube is not directed towards anyone in the room. Always point it towards a wall or other barrier.

5. Allow hot glassware and metal to cool sufficiently before handling them.

6. Never leave a substance being heated unattended. Turn off the burner when not in use.

COMMON LABORATORY GLASSWARE

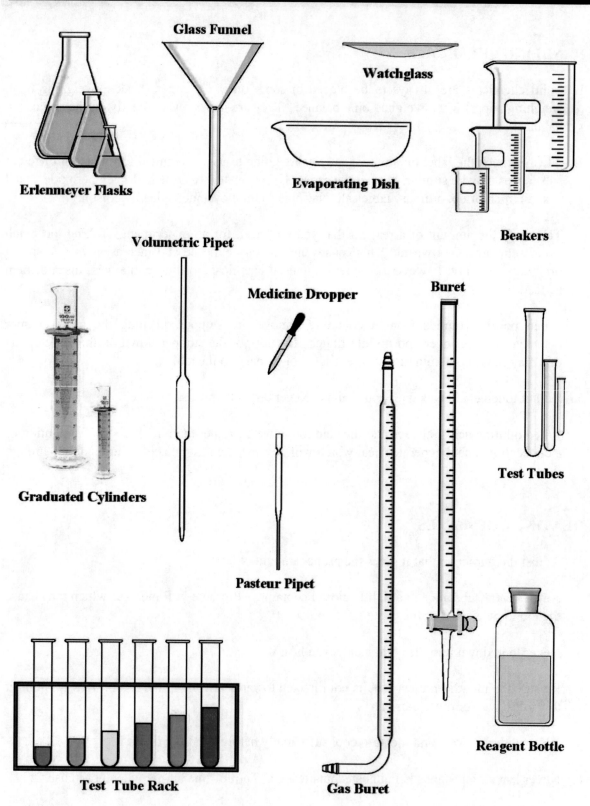

Glass Funnel

Watchglass

Erlenmeyer Flasks

Evaporating Dish

Beakers

Volumetric Pipet

Medicine Dropper

Buret

Graduated Cylinders

Test Tubes

Pasteur Pipet

Test Tube Rack

Gas Buret

Reagent Bottle

COMMON LABORATORY EQUIPMENT

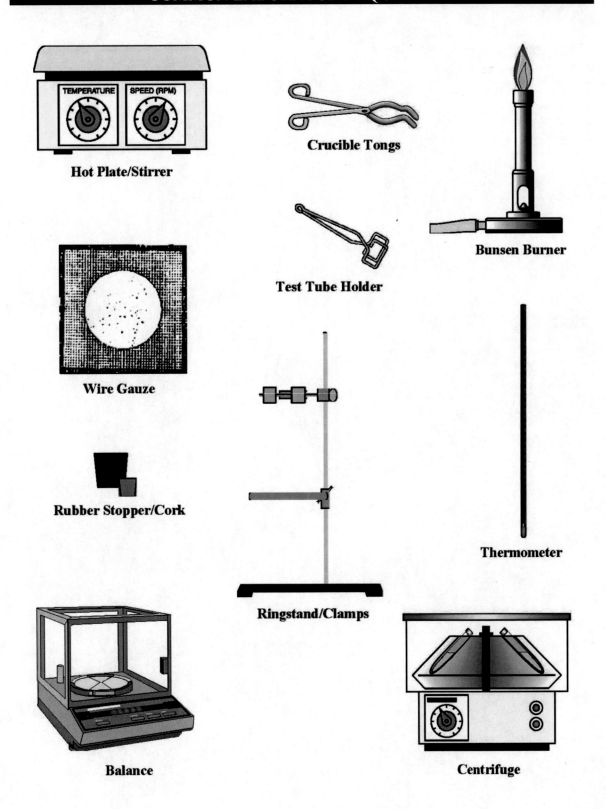

Hot Plate/Stirrer

Crucible Tongs

Bunsen Burner

Wire Gauze

Test Tube Holder

Rubber Stopper/Cork

Thermometer

Ringstand/Clamps

Balance

Centrifuge

EXPERIMENT # 1

INTRODUCTION TO THE BUNSEN BURNER
AND MAKING MEASUREMENTS

PURPOSE

To provide an introduction to the laboratory, including the proper use of the Bunsen burner. To learn techniques and acquire proficiency in using measuring devices.

INTRODUCTION

1. BUNSEN BURNER

The Bunsen burner is used frequently in the laboratory as a source of heat. The burner uses natural gas, which is composed of mostly methane (CH_4). Methane is a gas at room temperature, and its complete combustion with oxygen produces carbon dioxide and water vapor:

$$CH_4 + 2\,O_2 \rightarrow CO_2 + 2\,H_2O$$

If insufficient oxygen is present, carbon monoxide or carbon, as soot, may be produced.

$$2\,CH_4 + 3\,O_2 \rightarrow 2\,CO + 4\,H_2O$$

$$CH_4 + O_2 \rightarrow C + 2\,H_2O$$

This burner is designed so that its fuel may be mixed with the correct amount of air to yield the maximum amount of heat. In order to use this burner properly and safely, it is essential that you understand its construction and the adjustments that can be made.

The principal parts of the burner are: **gas inlet**, **nozzle**, **air vents**, **needle valve**, **barrel**, **base** and **hose**. The quantity of gas admitted to the burner is controlled by the needle valve, while the air needed for combustion is admitted at the air vents around the bottom of the barrel. The air is controlled by turning the barrel so as to make the air holes larger or smaller.

Always open the desk outlet valve fully and regulate the gas supply to the burner by the needle valve. Always extinguish your burner by turning off the desk outlet valve and then close the needle valve and barrel.

1

2. MAKING MEASUREMENTS

When a measurement is made in the course of an experiment it should be recorded to the correct number of significant digits. Values that are obtained from as digital output such as the mass on an electronic balance should include all the digits since they are all considered significant digits. If you are using a measurement device with a scale that must be read by eye then you should examine the scale attempting to make a measurement in order to determine the value of the scale markings. If the scale is marked with ten increments between digits then you should record one decimal place beyond the decimal place of the scale markings. For example, suppose that you were told to measure the length of the arrow below, using the centimeter ruler shown.

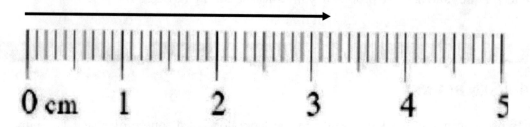

The arrow is clearly between 3 and 4 cm. The markings between digits each correspond to 0.1 cm. Therefore all the lengths measured with this ruler should be recorded to the second decimal place. To record the last decimal place in a measurement you must estimate whether the object is 1/10, 2/10 3/10 etc., between markings. One viewer may estimate the arrow to be 1/10th of the way between 3.20 and 3.30 so the length would be recorded as 3.21 cm. Most of viewers would estimate the length to be between 3.20 and 3.22. Notice that the viewer that estimates 3.20 cm as the length includes the final zero in his measurement to indicate that it is a significant digit.

If the scale you are reading is not marked in divisions of 10 the procedure for reading it to the correct number of significant figures is described in Appendix A. This is often the case when reading a ruler in units of inches. Sometimes glassware is also not marked in divisions of ten.

Values that are recorded using the rules of significant figures described above are generally considered to have an uncertainty of about +/- 1 digit in the last decimal place recorded. For instance, if a temperature is recorded with a thermometer that has marking of 1 degree Celsius the temperature would be recorded to the first decimal place after the decimal. A temperature such as 7.4 degrees recorded with this thermometer would be expected to be +/- 0.1 degrees or in other words within the range 7.3-7.5 degrees Celsius.

3. MEASUREMENT TECHNIQUES

Mass

Your instructor will demonstrate the use of the electronic balance in the laboratory. The balance is turned on and tared to zero. The object is placed on the pan, the windows are closed and the mass is read from the digital display in front. Masses can be read to a precision of 0.001 gram (1 mg) on these balances.

Solid chemicals are never placed directly on the pan. They are always placed either in a weighing boat or in a suitable container, and the mass obtained by difference. Liquids, of course, must be placed in a beaker, flask or graduated cylinder.

Volume

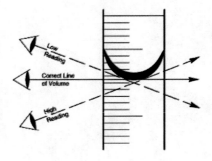

The volume of a liquid is determined by placing it in a graduated cylinder and reading the bottom of the meniscus (the curved surface the liquid takes), with the cylinder on a flat surface and at eye level. Remember you should record one decimal beyond the markings on the scale you are reading if the scale is marked in division of ten between digits. If the glassware is not marked in divisions of ten see Appendix A for detailed instructions on recording the number of significant figures.

PRE-LAB ASSIGNMENT

1. Record the length of the object below to the correct number of significant figures in units of centimeters.

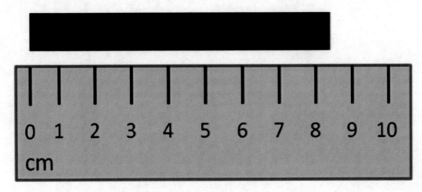

Length _____ cm

2. Based upon the rules of significant figures what range of values do you expect the length of the object in question 1 to be within?

3. Record the volume in the graduated cylinder below to the correct number of significant figures. You may wish to refer to appendix A.

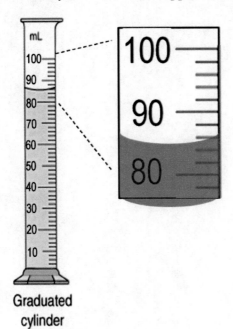

Graduated cylinder

Volume = _____ mL

EXPERIMENTAL PROCEDURE

1. BUNSEN BURNER

- Examine the Bunsen burner. Identify the gas inlet nozzle, air vents, needle valve, barrel, hose and desk outlet valve. Note the function of each on the data table.
- Attach the gas hose to the desk outlet valve. Close the needle valve completely by turning it counterclockwise until it is finger tight. Adjust the barrel so the air vent is "just" open (about one turn). Be sure the burner base is flat on the table.
- Note the off/on positions of the desk outlet valve. Open the desk outlet valve completely.
- Open the needle valve by a few turns. Light a match and hold the lit match to the side of the top of the barrel to light the burner.
- Close the barrel by turning it clockwise. Note the color and shape of the flame. This is called a **luminous flame.** This is a cooler type of flame and is rarely used in lab.
- Adjust the flame by turning the barrel counterclockwise, thus opening the air vents slowly until you have a pale blue flame. Note the color and shape of the flame. This is a warm flame and will sometimes be used in lab.
- Continue to adjust the flame by further opening the air vents slowly until you have a pale blue flame with a bright blue center or "inner cone". Note the color and shape of the flame. This is called a **non-luminous flame.** This type of flame is most often used in lab. It is a very hot burning flame.
- Continue to open the barrel until the air vents are wide open. Note that when too much oxygen is introduced to the gas mix, the flame is unstable.
- Adjust the barrel to get the inner cone back.
- Turn off the burner by shutting off the gas at the desk outlet valve. Then close the needle valve. Have your partner(s) go through the steps to relight the burner correctly.

When completed, have your instructor evaluate your competence in use of the burner and initial the report below.

INSTRUCTOR VERIFICATION: _____

2. TEMPERATURE OF BOILING WATER

Setup the hot water bath apparatus using a 50 mL beaker as shown below in Figure 1.

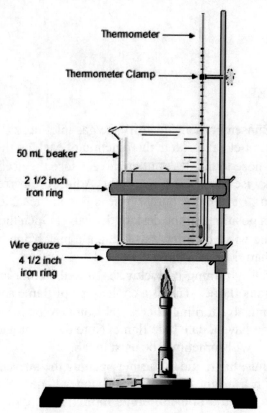

Figure 1. Hot water bath apparatus.

The bath should contain approximately 35 mL of water. Use a thermometer clamp to position the thermometer. The 4 ½ inch iron ring should be used to hold the wire gauze. The 2 ½ inch iron ring should be used as a safety ring to prevent the beaker from being knocked over. Be sure to adjust the height of the ring holding the wire gauze so that the inner cone of a properly adjusted Bunsen Burner flame will be focused on the wire gauze supporting the beaker (approximately 6 cm between the top of the Bunsen Burner and the wire gauze). Light and adjust the Bunsen Burner to heat the water bath vigorously.

While the water is being heated, tare the scale with a weighing boat. Using a scoopula place *approximately* 10 grams of sodium sulfate in the boat; any mass in the range of 9.5-10.5 grams is acceptable.

When the water begins boiling vigorously record the temperature as the *temperature of boiling water* on the data table. Be sure to read the thermometer to the correct number of significant figures. Next add several boiling chips to the water bath. Record your observations of the bath upon addition of the boiling chips in the space provided on the data table. Read the thermometer and record the temperature on the data table as the *temperature of the water bath after the addition of boiling chips*. Add approximately 10 grams of sodium sulfate you weighed earlier to the water bath. Stir it with the stirring rod if necessary until it all dissolves. When the solution begins boiling vigorously again, read the thermometer and record the temperature on the data table as the *temperature of the water bath after addition of sodium sulfate.*

Turn off the Bunsen burner and allow the beaker to cool on your bench top while you perform the rest of the experiment. Before you clean up for the day, make observations of the contents of the beaker after it has cooled to room temperature. The contents of the beaker may be washed down the sink with running water.

3. LENGTH MEASUREMENT

Use a ruler to measure the thickness of your lab manual from the first page of Experiment 1 to the last page of Experiment 14 in centimeters (cm). Be sure to record your result to the correct number of significant figures. (Estimate one digit between graduations.)

4. MASS MEASUREMENT

Your instructor will demonstrate and explain the use of the aspirator valves referred to in the procedure below.

1. From the laboratory cart obtain the apparatus to be evacuated. It is a stoppered vacuum flask that has been fitted with a piece of vacuum hose, which has a pinch clamp on it. It must be completely dry inside and out before proceeding with the experiment.

2. Make sure the stopper is firmly inserted into the apparatus.

3. Tare the electronic balance, place the apparatus on the pan, and close the glass doors around the sample compartment. (Note: You may have to coil up the hose so that it does not contact the doors inside the balance while its mass is being measured)

4. Record the mass on the data table as the *mass of the apparatus before evacuation.*

5. Attach the rubber tubing of the apparatus onto one of the aspirator valves under the fume hoods. Squeeze the pinch clamp so that it is not pinching the rubber hosing. Turn on the water to the fastest flow rate that does not splash water on the flask or you.

6. Allow the water to run for about one minute.

7. Release the pinch clamp allowing it to pinch the tubing. Remove the tubing from the aspirator valve and shut off the water. Do not shut off the water until the hose is pinched by the clamp.

8. If your apparatus was wetted at all, dry it off thoroughly with a paper towel.

9. Tare the electronic balance, place the apparatus on the pan, and close the glass doors around the sample compartment. You may have to coil up the hose so that it does not contact the doors inside the balance while being weighed.

10. Record the mass of the apparatus on the data table as the *mass of the apparatus after evacuation*.

11. Calculate the mass of air removed from the apparatus by evacuation and enter it on the data table as the mass *of air evacuated from the apparatus*.

5. VOLUME MEASUREMENT

Part I

1. From the laboratory cart obtain *approximately* 5 mL of isopropyl alcohol in a 10 mL graduated cylinder.

2. Record the actual volume you obtained to the correct number of significant figures on the data table.

3. Place *approximately* 10 mL of water in a 50 mL graduated cylinder. Record the actual volume you obtained to the correct number of significant figures on the data table.

4. Pour the alcohol into the 50 mL graduated cylinder with the water and swirl to mix the contents.

5. Record the volume of the mixture on the data table.

Part II

1. Fill an 18 mm x 150 mm test tube up to the top with water and pour the contents carefully into a 50 mL beaker. Record the volume on the data table to the correct number of significant figures.

2. Transfer the contents of the 50 mL beaker from above to a 50 mL graduated cylinder. Record the volume on the data table to the correct number of significant figures.

3. Transfer the contents of the 50 mL graduated cylinder to a 250 mL graduated cylinder. Record the volume on the data table to the correct number of significant figures.

EXPERIMENT # 1
INTRODUCTION TO THE BUNSEN BURNER
AND MAKING MEASUREMENTS
LABORATORY REPORT

1. BUNSEN BURNER

Briefly describe the function of the Bunsen burner parts

Gas inlet nozzle	
Air vents	
Needle valve	
Barrel	
Hose	
Desk outlet valve	

2. TEMPERATURE OF BOILING WATER

Temperature of boiling water	°C
Observations of boiling water bath after addition of boiling chips	
Temperature of the boiling water bath after the addition of boiling chips	°C
Temperature of the boiling water bath after addition of sodium sulfate	°C
Observations of sodium sulfate–water bath after cooling	

3. LENGTH MEASUREMENT

Thickness of 14 experiments in the laboratory manual	cm
Divide the thickness of 14 experiments in your lab manual by the number of pieces of paper measured to obtain the thickness of one page. Be sure to express your answer to the correct number of significant figures. Show your calculations below. Thickness of one page of your lab manual	cm
Convert the thickness of one page of your lab manual from units of centimeters into units of meters. 1 centimeter = 10^{-2} meters. Show calculations below Thickness of one page of your lab manual	m
Convert the thickness of one page of your lab manual from units of meters into units of micrometers. 1 micrometer = 10^{-6} meters. Show calculations below. Thickness of one page of your lab manual	µm

4. MASS MEASUREMENT	
Mass of apparatus before evacuation	g
Mass of apparatus after evacuation	g
Mass of air evacuated from apparatus	g

5. PART I: VOLUME MEASUREMENT	
Volume of isopropyl alcohol	mL
Volume of water	mL
Volume of isopropyl alcohol-water mixture	mL

6. PART II: VOLUME MEASUREMENT	
Contents of a large test tube in a 50 mL beaker	mL
Above contents measured in a 50 mL graduated cylinder	mL
Above contents measured in a 250 mL graduated cylinder	mL

EXPERIMENT # 2

MASS, VOLUME, AND DENSITY

PURPOSE

To determine the density of several liquids and solids; calculate percent errors.

INTRODUCTION

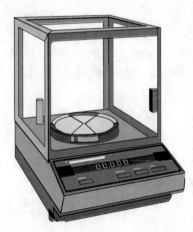

The density of a substance at a specific temperature is an intensive physical property. Such a property is one that is useful for identification. Yet, it is independent of the size of the sample used. Neither mass, the quantity of matter in an object, nor volume, the amount of space occupied by an object, separately aid in the identification of a substance. However, the ratio of an object's mass to its volume is a characteristic that may help to distinguish between different substances. The formula for density (D) is

$$D = \frac{M}{V} \qquad (1)$$

where M = mass and V = volume

To determine the density of a substance, we need to therefore determine both the mass and the volume of a sample of the material.

1. PRECISION

Precision indicates how close together or how repeatable a measured set of values are. A precise measuring device will give very nearly the same result each time it is used.

The precision of a set of data is often reported as the range of values observed, which is the difference between the highest and lowest values. The smaller the range the more precise the data set. For example see the data below.

More Precise		Less Precise	
Trial #1	Mass (g)	Trial #2	Mass (g)
1	100.00	1	100.10
2	100.01	2	100.00
3	99.99	3	99.88
4	99.99	4	100.02
Average	100.00	Average	100.00
Range	0.02	Range	0.22

The rules of significant figures predict the precision of a measurement will be about +/- 1 digit in the last decimal place that is significant. This corresponds to a range of three digits in the last decimal place. For instance if the temperature of an object was recorded as 10.2 °C the expect range could be expressed as 10.2 +/- 0.1 degree or 10.1 to 10.3 °C.

2. ACCURACY

Accuracy indicates how close a measurement is to the true or accepted value. For example, we'd expect a balance to read 100 grams if we placed a standard 100 g weight on the balance. If it does not, then the balance is inaccurate.

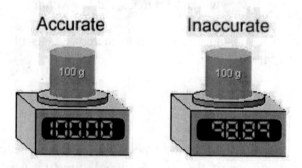

If a value is measured and its range based upon the rules of significant figures includes the accepted value then the measurement can be said to be accurate. For instance, standard masses can be purchased to test the accuracy of measurements that are made with the laboratory balances. If a standard has an accepted mass of 100.000 grams, and its mass was determined experimentally to be 100.1 grams then the experimental value is accurate. The reason it is considered accurate is that a measurement of 100.1 grams implies a range of values 100.0-100.2 grams, which includes the accepted value for the mass. If the experimental value was 99.8 grams the measurement would not be considered accurate because the range of possible values 99.7-99.9 does not include the accepted value.

PERCENT ERROR

Percent error calculations are used to determine how close to the true values, or how accurate, the experimental values really are. The value that the student determines is called the observed value, or the **experimental value**. A value that can be found in reference tables is usually called the true value, or the **accepted value**. The **percent error** can be determined using the equation below:

$$\text{Percent Error} = \frac{\left|(\text{experimental value} - \text{accepted value})\right|}{\text{accepted value}} \times 100\% \qquad (2)$$

For many experiments, a percent error of 5% or less is generally considered acceptable.

In this experiment you will determine experimental density values for various samples and calculate the percent error in your values using Equation 2. The accepted densities you will need for these calculations, as well as the pre-laboratory assignment, are all in Table 1.

LIQUIDS		SOLIDS	
Gasoline	0.730 g/mL	Aluminum	2.70 g/mL
Mercury	13.534 g/mL	Brass	8.14 g/mL
Methanol	0.791 g/mL	PVC	1.47 g/mL
Water	0.998 g/mL	Tecaform	1.41 g/mL
Osmium	22.6 g/mL	Gold	19.1 g/mL

Table 1. Densities of selected substances

PRE-LAB ASSIGNMENT

Show calculations clearly for any numerical problems.

1. What is the density of a solid if a sample weighing 55.234 grams raises the water level in a graduated cylinder from 18.6 mL to 25.7 mL?

2. Two groups of students perform an experiment to determine the density of gold. Each group performs the experiment three times; their results are summarized below:

                       GROUP A: 13.3 g/mL, 13.1 g/mL, 13.2 g/mL

                       GROUP B: 16.2 g/mL, 23.1 g/mL, 18.3 g/mL

(a) Find the average value for each group:

   GROUP A: GROUP B:

(b) Which group had the more accurate average result? Explain.

(c) Which group had the more precise average result? Explain.

(d) Find the range for each group:

GROUP A: GROUP B:

(e) How do the ranges for each group compare to the predicted range based on the rules of significant figures?

(f) Calculate the percent error for group A's average result.

EXPERIMENTAL PROCEDURE

1. **Density of a Liquid.** Place between 35 and 40 mL of methanol into a 50-mL graduated cylinder, and read the volume to the nearest 0.1 mL. Place a small watchglass on a clean dry 150-mL beaker. Put the watchglass and the beaker on the balance pan, and tare the balance to zero. Remove the beaker and watchglass. Transfer the methanol from the graduated cylinder into the beaker, and cover it with the watchglass. Place the beaker, watchglass and methanol on the balance pan, and record the mass of the methanol on the data table. When the procedure is completed, pour the used methanol into the bottle labeled "Used Methanol." Repeat this procedure using water in place of methanol.

From your experimental data calculate the densities of methanol and water. Record these values on the data table. Be sure to show your calculations in the space provided. Using your experimental density values and the accepted density values in Table 1, calculate the percent error in your determination of the densities of methanol and water. Record these values on the data table.

2. **Density of a Solid**. Obtain a solid unknown and record its code on the data table. Tare the balance to zero. Place the solid unknown on the balance pan and record its mass on the data table. Place about 30 mL of water into a 50-mL graduated cylinder, and read the volume of water to the nearest 0.1 mL. Tilt the 50-mL graduated cylinder and gently slide the unknown solid into the cylinder to avoid splashing out any water. Tap and agitate the cylinder to dislodge any trapped air bubbles. Read the new liquid volume in the graduated cylinder. The increase in volume is the volume of the solid unknown. Calculate this value and record it on the data table. Show your calculations in the space provided. Repeat the experiment using a different solid unknown.

Calculate the density of each of the solid unknowns. After you have completed your calculations show them to your instructor and they will provide you with the accepted density values. Using the accepted and your experimental values for the density of each solid unknown, calculate the percent error in your measurements. Record these values on the data table.

When you have completed the experiment, return both solid unknowns.

EXPERIMENT # 2
MASS, VOLUME, AND DENSITY
LABORATORY REPORT

Show any calculations in the spaces provided. Express all answers to the proper number of significant figures.

DATA AND CALCULATIONS
1. DENSITY OF LIQUIDS

		Calculations
1.	Mass of methanol	_____ g
2.	Volume of methanol	_____ mL
3.	Experimental density of methanol	_____ g/mL
4.	Accepted density of methanol (from Table 1)	_____ g/mL
5.	Percent error	_____ %

		Calculations
1.	Mass of water	_____ g
2.	Volume of water	_____ mL
3.	Experimental density of water	_____ g/mL
4.	Accepted density of water (from Table 1)	_____ g/mL
5.	Percent error	_____ %

DATA AND CALCULATIONS
2. DENSITY OF SOLIDS

Solid unknown code [   ]   *Calculations*

1. Mass of solid unknown   _____ g

2. Volume of solid unknown   _____ mL

3. Experimental density   _____ g/mL

4. Accepted density   _____ g/mL
    (from instructor)

5. Percent error   _____ %

Solid unknown code [   ]   *Calculations*

1. Mass of solid unknown   _____ g

2. Volume of solid unknown   _____ mL

3. Experimental density   _____ g/mL

4. Accepted density   _____ g/mL
    (from instructor)

5. Percent error   _____ %

POST-LAB QUESTIONS

1. For each of the following experimental errors clearly state if the error would increase, decrease or have no effect on the density values you determined in today's experiment. You *must* explain your reasoning.

   (a) Some methanol evaporated after the volume was measured, but before the mass was determined

   (b) Some air bubbles were stuck to the solid unknown when the total volume of the solid and water was measured.

   (c) Instead of using the volume of the solid in the calculation of the density the volume of the solid and water was used.

2. Would the experimental density values *you determined* in this experiment be more precise if you changed the procedure and weighed your samples to 0.0001 g instead of 0.001 g? You *must* explain your reasoning.

EXPERIMENT # 3
INTRODUCTION to PHYSICAL PROPERTIES

PURPOSE

To classify compounds as ionic or molecular compounds based upon the physical properties of melting point and conductivity, and to classify compounds as polar, of intermediate polarity, or non-polar based upon their solubility in oil, isopropyl alcohol, and water.

INTRODUCTION

A **physical property** of a substance is one that does not require changing the substances identity in order for it to be observed. For example, freezing a substance does not change its chemical identity. Therefore, the temperature at which a substance freezes is a physical property of the substance. A **chemical property** requires that the substance change its chemical identity in order for it to be observed. For instance, the ability of iron to undergo rusting is a chemical property because in order to observe it iron must be undergoing a chemical change, the formation a new compound, iron oxide. Evidence of a chemical change is often a change in the physical properties of a sample. For example, the color of a substance is a physical property because we can observe it without changing the substances chemical identity. When the chemical change of iron rusting occurs we observe the change in the color of an iron sample from metallic silver to the orange-brown color of rust.

When a substance dissolves in a liquid the resulting mixture is referred to as a **solution**. The liquid that the solution was formed from is called the **solvent** and the substance that dissolved is called the **solute**. If a substance will dissolve in a solvent it is said to be **soluble** in that solvent. Whether or not a substance is soluble in a solvent is a physical property, because when it dissolves the chemical identity of the substance is not changed. Oil and water display the physical property of *not* being soluble in each other. Even if a mixture of oil and water is shaken or stirred for a long period of time, after being allowed to sit, the mixture will separate into two layers with the less dense liquid forming the top layer.

The temperature at which a compound melts (changes from solid to liquid) is referred to as its **melting point** and is a physical property. Pure water is a very poor conductor of electricity, but *some* solutes can form aqueous solutions which will readily conduct electricity. The ability of a substance to cause aqueous solutions to conduct electricity when it dissolves is another example of a physical property. The physical properties of melting point and the ability to form conductive aqueous solutions are different for ionic and molecular compounds. Ionic compounds tend to have much higher melting points, typically greater than 300°C. In contrast, molecular compounds have melting points less than 300 °C. When ionic compounds dissolve in water the aqueous solutions formed will conduct electricity well. *Most*, molecular compounds that are soluble in water, form solutions that are either poor, or non-conductors of electricity.

Scientists often analyze data by creating categories for different types of observations that are made. A *Venn diagram* is a way to visually represent all the similarities and difference in such data. The advantage of a Venn diagram is that because it is a visual presentation of the data it allows all the data to be considered at once. For instance, the Venn diagram below summarizes all the observations about a chemistry class. In this example class there were 24 students, of which 18 were female and 6 were male. There were seven students in the class that wore glasses, and two of them were male. The Venn diagram below summarizes all this information. It can be very useful in simplifying seemingly complex questions. For instance, how many female students that wear glasses were in the class? The answer was not part of the given information, but it can be easily determined from the Venn diagram. The total number of students that were female is 18 because that is the total number inside the "female" circle (13 + 5). The total number of students that wore glasses is 7 (5 + 2) because that is the total in the "wears glasses" circle. The number of students that were female *and* wore glasses was five because that is the number in the region where female and wears glasses circles overlap.

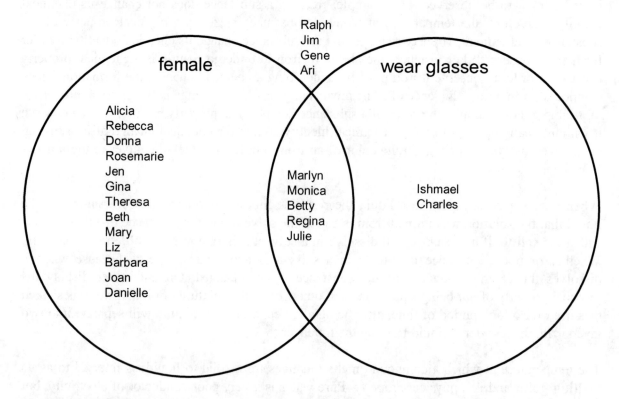

In Part 2 the physical properties of melting point and the ability to form conductive aqueous solutions will be determined for five compounds. Based upon these properties each compound will be classified as an ionic or molecular compound. One Venn diagram will be constructed for the properties "aqueous solution conducts electricity well" and "high melting point". Compounds that share both of these properties will be classified as ionic compounds. A second Venn diagram will be constructed for the properties "aqueous solution conducts electricity poorly" and "low melting point". Compounds that share both of these properties will be classified as molecular compounds.

When they are used as solvents oil and water tend to dissolve different *types* of substances. Most substances that dissolve in water do *not* dissolve in oil, and most substances that dissolve in oil do *not* dissolve in water. Substances which are soluble in water, but not soluble in oil are said to be **polar**. Substances that are soluble in oil, but not soluble in water, are said to be **non-polar**. Substances that are soluble in both oil and water can be described as having a polarity that is intermediate between oil and water.

A rough guideline for predicting the solubility of a substance in a solvent is often stated as "like dissolves like". It means that solutes tend to be soluble in solvents that have a similar polarity. For instance, acetic acid is considered a polar substance because it is soluble in water and not soluble in oil. The "like dissolves like" rule tells us that most polar substances that will dissolve in water will also dissolve in acetic acid because acetic acid and water are both polar. Similarly most non-polar substances will dissolve other non-polar compounds.

Some compounds such as isopropyl alcohol are soluble in both oil and water. These compounds have a polarity that is intermediate between oil and water. If isopropyl alcohol is used as a solvent substances that it dissolves best in it have a polarity that is intermediate between the polarity of oil and water.

In Part 1 of this experiment five compounds will be classified as polar, non-polar, or having an intermediate polarity based on their solubility in oil, water, and isopropyl alcohol.

Solvent	Polarity
Acetic Acid	Most Polar
Solution of water and sodium chloride	
Water	
Isopropyl Alcohol	**Decreasing polarity** ↓
Acetone	
Oil	
Benzene	Least Polar

Table 1. Some common solvents ranked in order of their polarity.

PRE-LAB ASSIGNMENT

1. A compound is found to have a melting point of 175 °C. One spatula scoop of the compound dissolves in water, but not in corn oil. The solution of the compound in water is found to be a poor conductor of electricity.

   (a) Explain how you would use this data to categorize this compound as molecular or ionic compound.

   (b) Explain how you would use this data to categorize this compound as a polar or non-polar compound.

2. Based upon the "like dissolves like" rule would you predict the compound of question 1 be more soluble in acetone or water? Explain why. You may wish to refer to Table 1.

PART 1: CLASSIFICATION OF COMPOUNDS BASED ON SOLUBILITY IN OIL, WATER, OR ISOPROPYL ALCOHOL

1. From the laboratory cart obtain the five compounds to be tested: pinacol, 2-napthol, cinnamic acid, 2,6-diaminohexanoic acid (lysine), and potassium chloride. Also obtain isopropyl alcohol, mineral oil, three disposable droppers, and five small test tubes with rubber stoppers.
2. Label the test tubes 1-5 with a pencil by writing in the white frosted area on the test tube.
3. Transfer one small spatula scoop of the each compound into the numbered test tubes as shown below.

> Test Tube 1 – pinacol
> Test Tube 2 – 2-napthol
> Test Tube 3 – cinnamic acid
> Test Tube 4 – 2,6-diaminohexanoic acid (lysine)
> Test Tube 5 – potassium chloride

4. Transfer one eyedropper full of mineral oil into each of the test tubes.
5. Place a lid on each test tube and shake vigorously.
6. Record your observations about the solubility of each compound in mineral oil on the data table.
7. Dispose of the contents of each test tube in the chemical waste container and clean them using soap and water.
8. Repeat steps 2-7 using isopropyl alcohol instead of mineral oil.
9. Repeat steps 2-6 using deionized water instead of mineral oil. **Do not dispose of these solutions!** Save them for Part 2.
10. Classify each compound as polar, non-polar, or of an intermediate polarity based on its solubility in mineral oil, water or isopropyl alcohol. If a compound is only soluble in mineral oil classify it as non-polar. If a compound is only soluble in water classify it as polar. If a compound is soluble in only isopropyl alcohol or is soluble in two solvents (mineral oil and isopropyl alcohol or water and isopropyl alcohol) classify it as having an intermediate polarity. Record your classification in Part 1 of the data table.

Save the samples with water as the solvent for Part 2

PART 2: CLASSIFICATION OF COMPOUNDS BASED ON CONDUCTIVITY AND MELTING POINT

The Conductivity Apparatus. The apparatus, as shown below, consists of a pair of solid brass probes connected to a battery-powered state-of-the-art electronics circuit. The display contains ten discrete multi-colored LEDs, and twenty levels of measurement using the high and low display settings. When a conductor is introduced between the two electrodes, the circuit is complete and the LEDs will cascade to a final reading. The "HIGH" circuit allows measurement of greater conductivities than the "LOW" circuit. The higher the number of the LED reading on either circuit the higher the conductivity of the sample. All LED Dx "HIGH" readings (values between 1 and 10 when the HIGH button is depressed) indicate that the sample is a strong electrolyte because it forms aqueous solutions that **conduct electricity well.** LED Dx "LOW" readings (values obtained when the LOW button is depressed) between 6 and 10 indicate that the sample weak electrolyte because it forms aqueous solutions that **conduct electricity poorly.** LED Dx "LOW" readings between 1 and 5 indicate that the sample is a is a non-electrolyte and forms aqueous solutions that **do not conduct electricity.**

INSTRUCTIONS for RCI–Dx Conductivity Meter

Using an eyedropper transfer some of the sample to be tested into a well in the spot plate. Avoid allowing solutions in different wells to mix by taking care to not overfill the well. Immerse the electrodes of the conductivity meter into the well of the spot plate. Depress the "HIGH" button waiting to see if any LEDs light. If some LEDs light wait until cascading stops and record the numerical LED reading indicating "high scale" as well as the numeric value. If the meter does not indicate any reading on the high scale depress the low scale reading. If some LEDs light wait until cascading stops and record the numerical LED reading indicating "low scale" as well as the numeric value. If you are unable to achieve an LED reading, on either scale see your instructor.

To restore the probes surface to a new-like state polish them with fine steel wool.

1. Obtain a conductivity meter from the laboratory cart.
2. Test the conductivity of each of the five aqueous solutions prepared above and record the readings on Part 2 of the data table.

Note: The brass probes should be rinsed with distilled water and wiped dry after each sample measurement.

Melting Point Determination

1. Obtain five capillary tubes from the laboratory cart.
2. Using a spatula place a very small scoop of pinacol on a piece of weighing paper.
3. Press the open end of the capillary tube into the pinacol on the weighing paper until a small amount has been forced into the tube. An amount that fills only a few millimeters of the tube is enough.
4. Invert the tube so the open end points upward and gently tap the closed end on the tabletop to shake the compound to the bottom of the tube.
5. Place the tube in the melting point apparatus, turn on the electronic thermometer attached to the melting point apparatus, and place the heat setting on 5.
6. Watch the sample through the viewing lens while your partner monitors the temperature of the apparatus.
7. When the sample completely melts record this temperature in the data table as the melting point.

Note: As soon as the melting point has been recorded turn of the melting point apparatus so that the temperature does not continue to rise.

8. If the instrument reaches 300 °C and the compound has not melted record the melting point as "higher than 300 °C"
9. Turn off the heating element and allow the apparatus to cool to a temperature below the melting point just measured.
10. Repeat this procedure for the other four compounds in the following order: 2-napthol, cinnamic acid, 2,6-diaminohexanoic acid (lysine), and potassium chloride.
11. Classify each compound as a molecular or ionic compound based on its melting point and whether its aqueous solutions were conductive. If any compound does not fit in either category classify it as ambiguous. Record your classification in the data table.

EXPERIMENT # 4

SEPARATION OF A SAND-SALT MIXTURE

To utilize some physical properties to quantitatively separate and analyze a mixture of salt and sand.

INTRODUCTION

Pure substances are rarely found in nature. Usually they are obtained by isolating them from mixtures. The goal in the separation of mixtures is to obtain one or more of the components of the mixture without changing the identity of the substance(s). Therefore, separation of mixtures is usually achieved by *physical processes*. By using physical rather than chemical processes, we ensure that the chemical identity of the substances is not changed.

For example, morphine, the most powerful pain medication known to man, is found in nature as a component of the poppy plant. Eating even a large number of poppy plants or poppy seeds does not deliver enough morphine to alleviate pain. Morphine must be isolated as a pure substance in order to deliver the dosages necessary in order for it to be effective. Therefore the separation of morphine from the other compounds that make up the poppy plant is done by physical means so that the morphine is not changed into a new compound in the process.

In this experiment, an unknown mixture of salt and sand is separated into its components by first dissolving the salt in water to yield sand and a solution of salt in water, and then evaporating the water to leave dry salt behind. It is essential that each component be dried thoroughly so we are weighing that component alone and that the two components are completely separated.

The percent by mass of each component is calculated by the following equation:

$$\% \ component \ (by \ mass) = \frac{mass \ of \ component}{mass \ mixture} \times 100\% \qquad (1)$$

This is a general technique for separating two components, only one of which is soluble in a given component. Solvent is added to the mixture, the insoluble component is washed with additional solvent several times, saving the washings, and the solvent is evaporated from each component.

Quantitative Analysis of an Unknown Sand-Salt Mixture.

Obtain an unknown sand-salt mixture. Be sure to note the unknown number on the data table. Weigh a clean dry 150-mL beaker, add a 3 to 5 gram sample of the mixture and weigh again. The difference between these two masses is the mass of mixture used. Also weigh a clean dry evaporating dish. All weighings are to be done on the electronic balance to the nearest 0.001 gram.

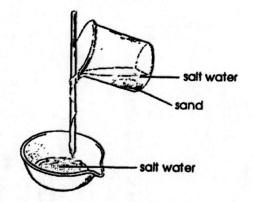

Add about 10 mL of distilled water to the sample of the mixture in the beaker and warm this gently to about 60-80°C, stirring it to permit all of the salt to dissolve. Let the sand settle and carefully decant the liquid down a stirring rod into the evaporating dish, as shown in Figure 1. Be careful not to allow any sand out of the beaker.

Figure 1. Decanting method for the sand-salt mixture

Repeat this process by adding a fresh 10 mL sample of distilled water to the beaker containing the sand. Again, all of the solution is transferred into the evaporating dish, and all of the sand remains behind in the beaker. Repeat this process a third time using a fresh 10 mL sample of distilled water. At this point, the beaker should contain only wet sand, and the evaporating dish should contain only an aqueous NaCl solution.

Heat the beaker containing the wet sand, gently at first, and then more vigorously to evaporate all of the water from the sand. The sides of the beaker, especially near the top, may also have to be heated to ensure that all of the water is evaporated off. When it is thoroughly dry, using crucible tongs remove the beaker from the heat, allow it to cool to room temperature and weigh it.

Assemble a hot water bath by filling approximately two-thirds of a 250-mL beaker with water. Place the beaker on a wire gauze on a ring stand, and place the evaporating dish on top of the beaker, as shown in Figure 2. Heat the beaker until the water in the evaporating dish appears to have completely evaporated. At this point remove the beaker using beaker tongs, place the evaporating dish on the wire gauze, and continue to heat it directly. Move the flame around the edges of the evaporating dish to avoid having any of the contents splatter out of the dish. Note the formation of the white salt crystals in the dish as the solution becomes more concentrated. When the salt is completely dry, let the dish cool completely, and determine **it's** mass. This gives us a second piece of data to obtain the percentage composition of the salt-sand mixture.

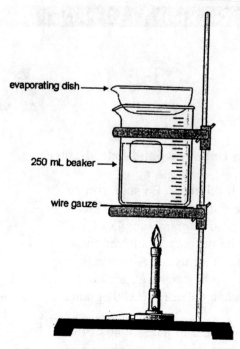

Figure 2. Water bath apparatus for evaporation of water from the salt-water mixture

EXPERIMENT # 5
DATA COLLECTION AND GRAPHING

PURPOSE

To learn how to collect and analyze data by constructing graphs.

INTRODUCTION

Data can consist of *qualitative observations* that do not involve numbers, such as "heat was released", "the color changed to blue", "bubbles formed after the acid was added", etc., or *quantitative data*, measurements that come in pairs of numbers, such as the temperature after 30 seconds was 25.9 °C, or the volume of the gas was 2.0 liters when the height of the column of liquid reached 30.06 cm, etc. Quantitative data can be presented in tables where the pairs of measurements form two columns, or in a graphical form where each measurement describes a distance along the x or y axis. Presenting data in a graph has the advantage of allowing trends to be observed quickly by considering all the data at a single glance. Graphs also allow estimates to be made of data that has not been collected by techniques called *extrapolation* or *interpolation*.

CONSTRUCTING A GOOD GRAPH

1. DECIDE WHICH QUANTITIES SHOULD GO ON THE X AND Y AXIS

In experiments where quantitative data is collected, one quantity is usually measured and the other is prepared in advance or scheduled to be collected at regular intervals. For instance, a set of solutions with different amounts of sugar could be prepared, and then measurements made to determine each solution's volume; or a substance could be burned, and the temperature measured every 30 seconds. The quantity that is measured is called the *dependent variable* and should be placed on the vertical or **y axis**. The quantity that is prepared or scheduled is called the independent variable, and it should be placed on the horizontal or **x axis**. So for the example of the sugar solutions, the amount of sugar should be on the **x axis** and the volume of the solution on the **y axis**. For the example of the substance being burned the time should be on the **x axis** and the temperature should be on the **y axis**. If the experiment were conducted differently, and instead of collecting temperature measurements every 30 seconds the time was measured with every one degree of temperature change, then the axis assignments would be reversed. Both experiments would produce graphs that conveyed the same relationship between the variables.

2. DECIDE HOW MUCH EACH BOX SHOULD COUNT

A good graph should make use of the majority of the available space, but also have a scale that has convenient sizes assigned to the boxes or scale ticks.

To calculate good sizes to assign to each box:

1) Count the number of boxes available along each axis.
2) Examine the data table and determine the largest and smallest values in each column. If the smallest value is close to zero replace that value by zero in the next step.
3) Subtract the smallest value from the largest value and divide the result by the number of boxes available along that axis.
4) Round the calculated box size *up* to the nearest number starting with the digits 1.0, 2.5, or 5.0.

For example, if a data table had temperatures that ranged from 12 °C to 45 °C, and the graphing region had 14 boxes available, the value per box for the temperature axis could be calculated as (45-12)/14 = 2.35 degrees C per box. This value would then be rounded to 2.5 °C per box.

3. LABEL THE AXIS AND SCALE

Each of the axes must be labeled with the dependent and independent variables names neatly printed parallel to the axis. The axis label should include units either in the description of the quantity or abbreviated in parentheses. For example a label could be written "Time in seconds" or "Time (s)".

Label the axis with text that is large enough to be legible at arms length, though not so large as to be visually distracting. The scale should be labeled in a slightly smaller text size, but should also be readable when held at arms length. The numbers on the scale should be marked periodically, but leave enough space so that the numbers are clearly separated. See good and bad examples below (Figures 1, 2, and 3) as a guide.

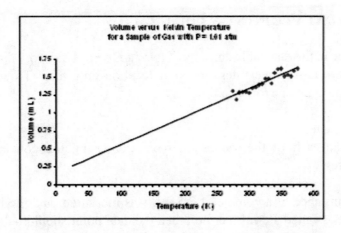

Figure 1. A graph with acceptable text size used on the axis labels

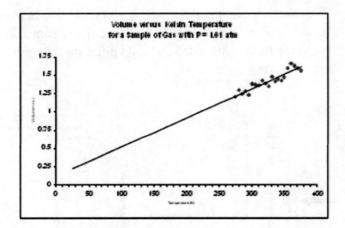

Figure 2. A graph with text that is too small used on the axis labels

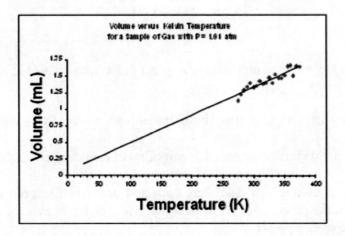

Figure 3. A graph with text that is too large used on the axis labels

4. LOCATE THE DATA POINTS ON THE GRAPH

Notice that each *row* in the data table consists of two numbers. The two values describe one point on the graph like two cross streets describe your location on a map. To enter the data into the graph work down the table one row at a time.

For each pair of values:

1) Locate each of the values on their axis using the conventions of significant figures.

   For instance, if a volume of 2.5 mL was measured, and the boxes along that axis were assigned 1.0 mL per box then the data point should be located by estimating the point 5/10 of the distance between 2.0 mL mark and the 3.0 mL mark along the volume axis (see Figure 4 below).

2) Use a T-square to locate the point where a vertical line heading up from this point on the **x axis** and a horizontal line heading right from this point on the **y axis** point would intersect. This is the one data point described by that *pair* of numbers (see Figure 4 below).

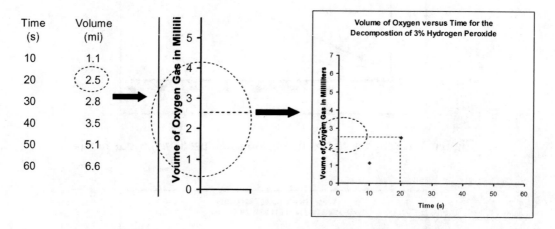

Figure 4. Steps for locating data points in a graph from values in a data table

3) Neatly and precisely mark this point with a symbol of your choice.

4) Repeat this procedure for each pair of numbers going down the data columns.

5) If other columns of data were collected under similar, but different conditions, repeat the procedure for this data, but use a different symbol to mark the location of these data points.

5. INTERPRET IF THE DATA IS LINEAR OR CURVED

The trends reflected in a set of data are interpreted and then used to decide if a hypothesis should be accepted or rejected. One hypothesis could be that the data points have a trend that forms a straight line. Another hypothesis could be that the data points have a trend that is curved. Deciding which trend fits your data constitutes a scientific interpretation of the data. In order to make a sensible interpretation always start by considering if the data could have a linear trend.

Using a straight edge and a pencil, draw a line that gets as close to as many of the data points as possible. The line should *not* be constructed to connect the first and last, or any other specific data points. The best line may come close to, but never intersect *any* data points.

If the data in some regions is *all* on one side of the line, and in another region is all on the other side of the line, as in Figure 5 below, the trend is probably *not* linear but curved instead. If the data follows a linear trend the points will be randomly distributed above and below the trend line like the data in Figure 6. If you determine the data has a linear trend then darken the pencil line or mark it with a sharp point pen using a straight edge. This trend line now represents the best estimate this data set can offer of the relationship between these two variables. In constructing it all of the data was considered. Just as repeating a single measurement and averaging the results will improve the quality of a measurement, a trend line represents an improvement in the quality of all the measurements used to construct it.

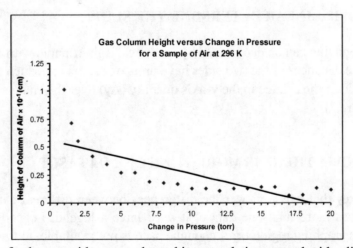

Figure 5. Example of a dataset with a curved trend incorrectly interpreted with a linear trend line

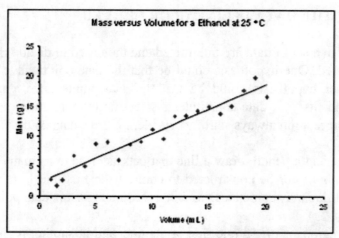

Figure 6. Example of a dataset with a linear trend correctly interpreted with a linear trend line

If you determine that the trend in the data is curved, then a curved trend line should be constructed to interpolate and/or extrapolate the data. This curved trend line should be drawn as close as possible to all the data points, though it is not necessary that it intersects *any* individual data points. You may construct a curved line using a flexible plastic ruler. To do this, hold the ruler in two hands with its *narrow edge* on the graph paper. Bend the ruler to follow the curve until it follows a path that stays as close as possible to all the data, and have your partner mark this curve with a pencil.

6. IF THE TREND IS LINEAR DETERMINE THE SLOPE

The slope of the trend line can be determined by drawing a right triangle with the trend line as the hypotenuse. The distances of the two sides have units of the axis to which they are parallel. The slope is the ratio of the change in the **y-axis** quantity (Δy) over the change in the **x-axis** quantity (Δx) (Figure 7).

7. ADD A LEGEND IF THERE IS MORE THAN ONE DATASET

The legend is the key that tells a viewer the differences between different data sets on the same graph. If a graph has more than one dataset it *must* have a legend. Legends can be placed in unused space in the graphing region or, if enough space is not available, to the right of the graph. To create the legend, make a list showing each symbol with the briefest possible description of the dataset placed to the right of it. To complete the legend, the list should be neatly enclosed in a box.

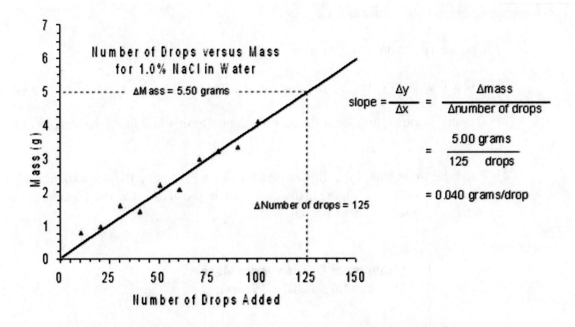

Figure 7. Determination of the slope of a linear trend line

8. GIVE THE GRAPH A TITLE

The title of a graph should be brief. It could simply state the quantities on the **x** and **y axis** and the conditions, such as "Temperature **vs** Time for the Reaction of Hydrochloric Acid with Sodium Hydroxide". The title should *not* be used as an opportunity to interpret or explain the data. If more than one graph has been created precede the title with "Graph 1.", "Graph 2." etc, so they may be referred to later simply as Graph 1 or Graph 2 instead of repeating the whole title. Finally, clean up all stray pencil marks with an eraser.

9. EXTRAPOLATION AND INTERPOLATION OF VALUES FROM A GRAPH

Once a trend has been determined, a graph can be used to determine values of the **x** or **y axis** quantities where no data was actually collected. If the estimate is to be made in a region between collected data points it is called *interpolation*. If the estimate is to made in a region beyond the values of any collected data it is called *extrapolation*.

For instance using a graph of mass versus volume for a substance, if one chooses a mass the graph can be used to determine the volume of that mass of substance by interpolation or extrapolation. Using the same graph, one could also choose a volume and estimate the mass of that volume of substance from the graph.

To extrapolate or interpolate a value from a graph:

1) Choose a point on either the **x or y axis**.

2) Use a T-square to draw a line from the selected point on the axis to the trend line.

3) Use the T-square to trace a line perpendicular to this line that intersects the other axis.

4) Read the value where this line strikes the other axis using the rules of significant figures as shown in Figure 8 below. This is the mass that corresponds to the initially selected number of drops.

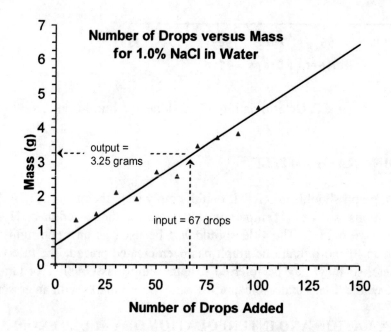

Figure 8. Determination of the mass of 67 drops by interpolation

10. LEAVING SPACE IN A GRAPH FOR EXTRAPOLATION

If a graph is going to be used for extrapolation more space must be left to extend the trend line. This can be done by increasing the quantity assigned to the boxes on each axis by the same factor. For instance, if extrapolation of data over twice the range was to be performed before constructing the graphs the box sizes on both axes should be multiplied by two.

Save this introduction, pages 1-8, to use as a reference in later experiments that require the construction of graphs.

PRE-LAB ASSIGNMENT

1. A series of measurements were made as a gas was formed in a chemical reaction. With every 1.0 mL increase in volume of gas produced, the total time elapsed was measured. If this data was graphed should time go on the x or y axis?

2. If the data below was to be graphed on paper that had 45 boxes available for both the x and y axis, and it was known that extrapolation would be performed over a range of temperatures 4 times larger than the range of the measured temperatures, what temperature would you assign to each box? Show your work.

Temperature (K)	Volume (mL)
275	1.27
280	1.30
285	1.23
290	1.26
295	1.32
300	1.29
305	1.32

PART 1

1. Clean, thoroughly rinse, and dry a 50 mL beaker, a 150 mL beaker, and an eyedropper. Place at least 10 mL of distilled water in the 150 mL beaker. Tare the analytical balance with the 50 mL beaker on it. Then, add *about* 10 drops of water, and record the mass along with the exact number of drops on the data table. The quality of the data will not depend on adding exactly 10 drops, but will depend on knowing exactly how many drops were added. There is no need to restart the experiment if more than 10 drops are accidentally added as long as the number of drops added is known. Without taring the balance again, repeat the addition of about 10 drops nine times, recording on the data table the total number of drops added to that point and the total mass in the beaker.

2. Prepare a soap solution by mixing 1 drop of soap in about 100 mL of water in a 150 mL beaker. Repeat the procedure of Step 1 using this soap solution instead of water.

PART 2

1. Using a 50 mL graduate cylinder measure *about* 5 mL of distilled water. It is not necessary to adjust the amount of water to get the exact volume. A volume *within* 1 mL is acceptable. Record the volume read off the graduate cylinder to the correct number of significant figures on the data table.

2. Place a clean dry 50 mL beaker on the analytical balance and tare the instrument. Add the measured volume of water to the beaker, and record its mass adjacent to the measured volume on the data table.

3. Discard the water from the graduate cylinder.

4. Repeat steps 1, 2 and 3 using *about* 10, 15, 20, 25, 30, 35, 40, and 45 mL of water.

Student Name_____ Partner's Name(s)_____

Date_____ Course/Section_____ Instructor_____

EXPERIMENT # 5
DATA COLLECTION AND GRAPHING
LABORATORY REPORT

DATA AND CALCULATIONS
PART 1

Record the total number of drops and the mass

Water		Water + Soap Solution	
Total Number Drops	Total Mass (g)	Total Number Drops	Total Mass (g)

Construct a graph of *Total Number of Drops versus Total Mass in grams* using the data for both water and soap solutions. Label this Graph 1. Attach this graph to this report.

DATA AND CALCULATIONS
PART 2

Record the volume and the mass

Volume (mL)	Measured Mass (g) (Accepted Value)	Calculated Mass (g) (Experimental Value)	Percent Error

1. Calculate the mass of each sample from the volume assuming a density of 1.00 gram/mL for water. Record the results on the data table above as the Calculated Mass.

2. Calculate the Percentage Error for each volume measurement, by assuming that the balance is calibrated and is therefore accurate. Therefore, the mass measured directly on the balance will be taken as the accepted value. The mass *calculated* from the volume will be taken as the experimental value. Record the percentage error on the data table in the same row as the volume and mass from which it was calculated.

3. Construct a graph of Percentage Error versus Volume in milliliters. When constructing this graph plan to extrapolate the volume down to 0.0 ml and 0.0% error. Label this Graph 2. Attach this graph to this report.

POST-LAB QUESTIONS

1. Based upon its units, explain the significance of the slope in Graph 1.

2. Using a T-square and pencil, determine the mass of 36 drops of water from Graph 1. Show any calculations used to determine the result.

3. Based on the trend in Graph 2, does the percent error increase or decrease as the volume measured with the graduate cylinder increases?

4. In science a 5% error is considered acceptable in many cases. Based upon the data in Graph 2, estimate the volume at which the percent error of the volume measured with the 50 mL graduate cylinder would be 5%.

66

EXPERIMENT # 6
CHROMATOGRAPHY

PURPOSE

To separate the components of a mixture using paper chromatography.

INTRODUCTION

Most compounds and elements are not found in nature in a pure form. Pure substances are usually obtained by isolating them from mixtures. For instance, sucrose (table sugar) can be isolated from the sugar cane plant which contains numerous other compounds. In other cases, substances are isolated from *reaction mixtures* that are created when chemical reactions are performed for the purpose of producing an element or compound. These mixtures can consist of the solvent in which the reaction was performed, some of reactants that failed to undergo reaction, or unwanted products that were formed in addition to the desired product. In this experiment a mixture will be separated. It will consist of the inks founds in a felt-tipped marker.

Most techniques to separate a pure substance from a mixture are based on differences in the physical properties of the substances. For instance, mixtures of liquids with different boiling points can be separated by distillation, which is based on the differences in the boiling points of the liquids. The liquid with the lower boiling point will evaporate more quickly when the mixture is heated. If the vapor is collected and re-condensed into a liquid it will contain *mostly* the liquid with the lower boiling point.

Chromatography is an approach to separating mixtures that is often applied to mixtures with many components. In **liquid chromatography** the mixture is added to a solid material called the **stationary phase** and then **eluted** or "washed out" with a liquid solvent called the **mobile phase**. Different substances have different tendencies to stick to the stationary phase; compounds that stick more strongly take a longer time to elute. All compounds have a different solubility in the **mobile phase**. The higher the solubility of a compound in the **mobile phase** the faster it will elute. The physical property that describes how fast elution occurs is called the R_f **value** of the compound or element. A compound's R_f value reflects how much the compound sticks to the **stationary phase,** *and* how soluble it is in the **mobile phase**. Components with large R_f values elute quickly; those with small R_f values elute slowly.

There are many different materials that can be used as the **stationary phase**. In this experiment the **stationary phase** will be chromatography paper. This is a heavy-weight paper that is more absorbent than conventional paper. It is also very porous, which causes it to readily draw in the solvent.

A wide variety of solvents and solvents mixtures can be used as the **mobile phase**. Determining the best **mobile phase** to use for a mixture usually involves some trial and error. The goal is to find a **mobile phase** in which each component of the mixture has a significantly different R_f value so that each will elute sequentially achieving good separation.

To separate a mixture by paper chromatography, the mixture is spotted towards the bottom of the chromatography paper. The paper is then placed in a container with just enough of the **mobile phase** to cover the bottom of the container. It is then covered to prevent evaporation of the **mobile phase**. As the paper slowly absorbs the solvent, the mixture is drawn up the paper. The *chromatogram* is allowed to elute until the liquid front gets close to the top of the paper at which point it is removed from the solvent and allowed to dry. Before the chromatogram dries a mark should be made with a pencil at the level the mobile phase reached.

One approach to deciding on a **mobile phase** that will achieve a good separation of a mixture is to use mixtures of two solvents as the mobile phase; one solvent which some of the components will be soluble in, and one solvent in which some will not be. The more soluble a component is in the mobile phase the faster it will elute. If the percentage of one solvent, in which some components are very soluble, is increased in the **mobile phase** those components will elute faster. After a series of chromatograms are run with mixtures containing different percentages of each solvent, the **mobile phase** that produces the greatest difference in R_f values is selected.

Features commonly seen in chromatograms

1) **Spreading out**. As compounds move up the chromatogram they spread out. Initially this is mostly seen along the direction the **mobile phase** is moving creating oblong spots. As the **mobile phase** reaches greater heights, movement up the paper slows down. As this happens, the samples spreading out to the left and right becomes more apparent, widening their oblong shape.

2) **Spots overlap**. If a chromatogram is eluted long enough, the spots will become completely separated. If the chromatogram is not eluted sufficiently to fully separate the components, the spots will overlap. The R_f values can be measured if overlapping circles can be estimated around each spot.

3) **Sample forms a half circle**. If a single component moves at the same rate as the **mobile phase**, the spot may appear to be a half circle. In this case the center of the spot is located at the liquid front itself making the R_f value one.

4) **Streaking**. If too much sample is placed on the chromatogram, or if one of the components is only slightly soluble in the **mobile phase**, the sample may form streaks. If a component forms a streak, no R_f value can be assigned to that component. If the other components form distinct spots they can be assigned R_f values.

5) **All the components move with the mobile phase liquid front**. If all of the components are very soluble in the eluting solvent they will all have R_f values close to one. This leads to very ineffective separation. The **mobile phase** should be changed to a mixture with a solvent in which the components are less soluble.

6) ***None* of the samples are moved by the mobile phase.** If all of the components are very insoluble in the eluting solvent, they will all have R_f values close to zero. This also leads to very ineffective separation. The solvent should be changed to a mixture with a solvent in which the components are more soluble.

How much sample should be used?

The ideal amount of sample is a compromise between two factors. If a very small amount of the mixture is used, components that are present in small percentages may not be visible. On the other hand, placing too large an amount of the mixture can cause some components to form streaks. Even if no streaking occurs, placing too much of the mixture will create larger spots that require longer elution times to become separated. The ideal amount of the mixture is the amount that is just enough so that each spot is visible. This will allow measurement of R_f for every component with the shortest elution time, and best separation. Determining the ideal amount of sample usually involves some trial and error. Several trials are usually run with different amounts of the mixture spotted. The trial with the smallest amount of the mixture in which all the components are visible has the ideal amount (Figure 1).

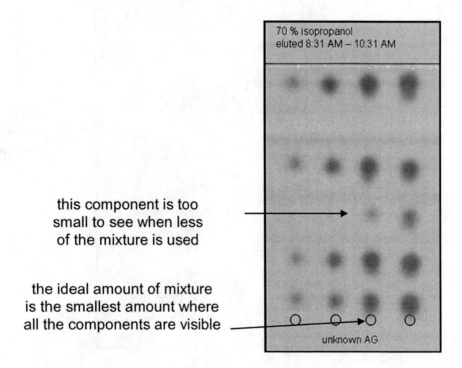

this component is too small to see when less of the mixture is used

the ideal amount of mixture is the smallest amount where all the components are visible

Figure 1. Eluted chromatogram prepared with different amounts of mixture

Measuring R_f values

To measure the R_f value from a chromatogram, use a pencil to mark the center of the circle where the mixture was originally spotted. Then, using a pencil, trace the outline of the region each spot reached. Locate and mark the center of the spot. Use a ruler to measure the distance this component traveled from the center of the mixture was spotted to the center of the point it reached. Use a ruler to measure the distance from the center of the point the mixture was spotted to the edge of the liquid front (Figure 2). Calculate R_f using Equation 1.

$$R_f = \frac{\text{distance sample traveled}}{\text{distance eluting solvent traveled}} \qquad (1)$$

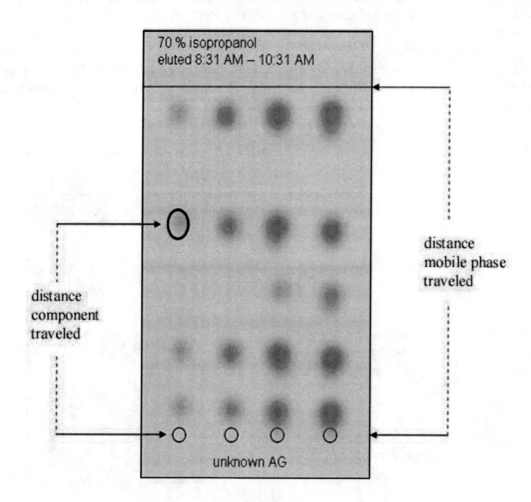

Figure 2. Distances measured to calculate R_f

| Student Name_____ | Course/Section_____ |
| Date_____ | Instructor_____ |

PRE-LAB ASSIGNMENT

1. What are the units on R_f?

    Cm

2. Using a ruler measure the R_f values for each of the components in the chromatogram below.

70 % isopropanol
eluted 8:31 AM – 10:31 AM

component 1

component 2

component 3

component 4

component 5

unknown AG

10.4 cm

Component	R_f
1	.817
2	.548
3	.356
4	.216
5	.115

3. A mixture was eluted with several different mobile phases. The R_f values measured in each mobile phase are shown below.

Component	R_f Values			
	Pure Water	50% Isopropanol	75% Isopropanol	100% Isopropanol
Blue	1.00	0.882	0.952	0.191
Red	0.973	0.675	0.924	0.113
Green	0.955	0.433	0.882	0.0414
Orange	0.0532	0.241	0.601	0.0391

Which mobile phase is the best for separating the components of the mixture? Why?

50% Isopropanol is the best for separation of components b/e it has an equal amount of distance between each other.

1. Obtain from the laboratory cart two pre-cut (9.5 cm × 9.5 cm) pieces of chromatography paper, a pencil, and a clear plastic chromatogram template. Using the template, mark the locations for six spots on one of the pieces of chromatography paper. Using a pencil, label this chromatogram "70% isopropyl alcohol" within 1 cm of the top of the chromatogram (the edge furthest from the spot locations). Write your initials in this area using a pencil.

2. Obtain from your instructor two pens or markers and record their numerical unknown codes on the data table. Using a pencil, write the first unknown code under the first three sample spots. Using a pencil, write the second unknown code under the second three sample spots.

3. Using the unlabeled piece of chromatography paper as scrap, practice creating spot sizes from less than one millimeter up to 2 millimeters in diameter.

4. When you are confident that you have developed good enough technique you are ready to begin spotting your chromatogram. Use the first marker to spot three samples of ink onto the chromatogram labeled 70% isopropanol. The first spot should be as small as possible (*less* than 1 mm). The second spot should be larger than the first (*about* 1 mm). The third spot should be about the size of the circle created using the template (*about* 2 mm) (Figure 3).

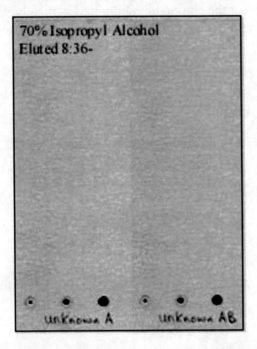

Figure 3. Chromatogram prepared with different sample loadings before elution.

5. In pencil, record the time and your initials in the area within 1 cm of the top of the chromatogram. Give your chromatogram to your instructor to place in the elution tank.

> Note to Instructors: The tank is designed so that each position has a double string crossing the tank for each chromatogram. Separate the two strings and place the chromatogram between the strings which will hold it gently in place during elution.

6. Your instructor will monitor the progress of the elution up the chromatogram and remove it when the mobile phase is about 1 cm from the top of the chromatogram.

7. Lay the chromatogram flat on a clean paper towel for a few seconds to absorb excess solvent. Do not leave it laying on a paper towel to dry.

8. Using a pencil, record the time the chromatogram was removed from the elution tank in the dry area towards the top of the chromatogram. Using a pencil, mark the height that the mobile phase reached on the chromatogram. This can be done while the bottom of the chromatogram is still drying.

9. Holding it from the edges, use a hair dryer or heat gun on a low setting to dry the chromatogram. Overheating the chromatogram may damage the sample spots making the chromatogram interpretation impossible.

> Caution: Avoid touching the barrel of the hair dryer or heat gun. It becomes hot enough to cause a burn.

10. Use a pair of scissors to cut the chromatogram in half vertically. Each half should contain the three lanes for one of the two markers. Each partner will analyze and submit one half of the chromatogram.

Student Name_____ Partner's Name(s)_____

Date_____ Course/Section_____ Instructor_____

EXPERIMENT # 6
PAPER CHROMATOGRAPHY
LABORATORY REPORT

DATA AND CALCULATIONS

After the chromatogram has thoroughly dried, examine the three lanes that contain the unknown sample. Using a pencil, circle each component in the lane with the smallest amount of sample in which it is visible. Visually locate the center of this circle or ellipse and mark it with a small spot. Also, make a small spot at the center of the circle into which the sample was spotted. Number the components on the chromatogram and enter these numbers on the data table. Use Equation 1 to measure the R_f value for each component and enter the value onto the data table. Staple the chromatogram in the designated area below.

Identify the letter code of your unknown marker by comparing your half of the chromatogram to the master chromatogram at your instructor's desk. Compare the number of spots, their color, and their R_f values when determining the identity of your unknown. Record the letter code from the master chromatogram to the right of your marker's numerical unknown code on the data table.

chromatogram eluted with 70% isopropanol

70% Isopropanol	
Component	**R$_f$**
Pheophytin	
Xanthophyll	
Chlorophyll A	
Chlorophyll B	
Lutein	

Letter code marker of unknown code	Numerical code from the master chromatogram that matches your unknown marker

POST-LAB QUESTIONS

1. Examine the three lanes in your half of the chromatogram. Which of these lanes has achieved the best separation? Explain your answer.

2. Paper chromatography was used to separate a mixture. Five chromatograms were prepared and each was eluted with a different mobile phase. The five mobile phases used were mixtures with different percentages of water and isopropanol. The following R_f values were obtained.

		R_f Values			
Component	Water	25% Isopropanol	50% Isopropanol	75% Isopropanol	100% Isopropanol
Blue	1.00	0.96	0.91	0.85	0.7
Red	0.99	0.91	0.72	0.52	0.31
Green	0.98	0.61	0.41	0.41	0.42
Orange	0.97	0.32	0.16	0.10	0.01

Prepare a graph of R_f value versus percentage of isopropanol in the eluting mixture. Assign a different symbol to each component of the mixture. Determine if each set of data represents a linear or curved trend and the construct an appropriate trend line for each set.

3. Based on the graph prepared for question 2, estimate the percentage of isopropanol that would achieve the best separation of all the components of this mixture. Hint: the best separation was *not* achieved with any of the percentages used in the five trials that the graph was based upon.

50% would be the best
separation

RF VS %

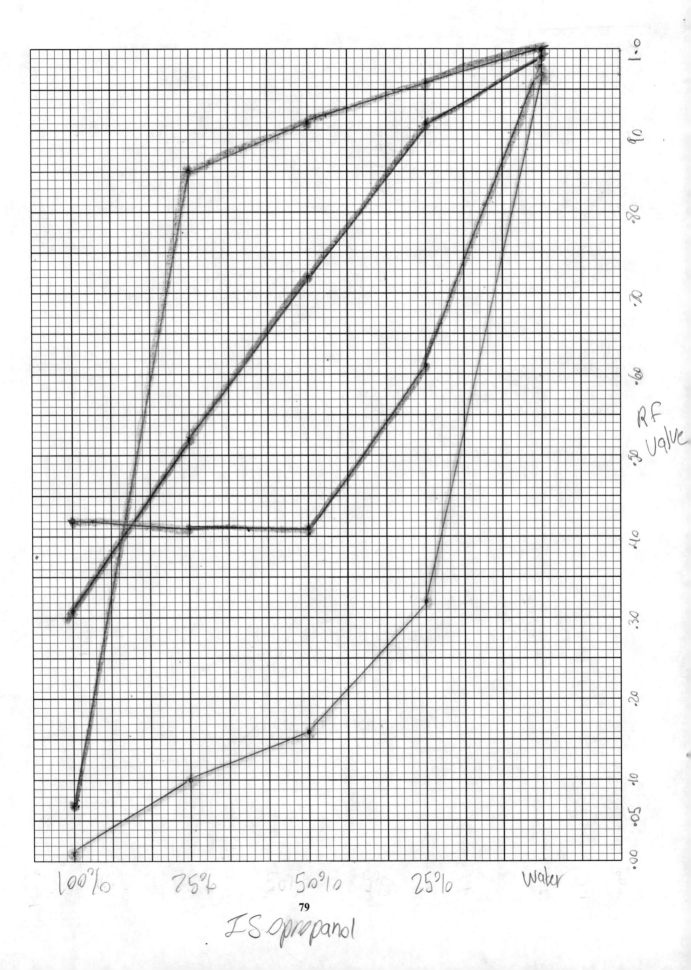

RF Value

100%   75%   50%   25%   water

Isopropanol

EXPERIMENT # 7

BOYLE'S LAW

To measure the volume of a sample of gas at different pressures; to use this data to determine the Boyle's Law constant for this sample of gas and to verify Boyle's Law.

INTRODUCTION

Boyle's Law states that for a given quantity of gas at a fixed temperature the product of its pressure and volume is constant.

$$P \times V = k \tag{1}$$

where P and V are the pressure and volume of the gas, respectively, and k is the Boyle's Law constant for this sample of gas at this temperature. Another way of stating this is that the volume of a gas is inversely proportional to its pressure at constant temperature.

In this experiment, the gas used will be a sample of air. It occupies the flask, the connecting tube and part of the buret, as shown in Figure 1. The volume occupied by the air in the connecting tube is small compared to the volume in the flask and buret and it will be neglected in this experiment. The pressure of the gas is adjusted by raising or lowering the leveling bulb. In the position shown, the gas pressure is greater than the atmospheric pressure. A measure of the difference in pressure is the difference in heights between the leveling bulb and the water level in the buret. We will measure all heights from the laboratory bench. Note that if the leveling bulb is below the bench level, h_2 has a negative value.

The gas volume is measured in mL and is the sum of the volume of gas in the buret and the flask. The gas pressure is more complicated to calculate. We will measure pressure in cm of H_2O. To convert mm Hg (torr) into cm H_2O: (1) divide by ten to change from mm to cm, (2) multiply by 13.6, the specific gravity of Hg to convert from heights of Hg to heights of H_2O.

$$cm\ H_2O = mm\ Hg \times \frac{1\ cm}{10\ mm} \times \frac{13.6\ cm\ H_2O}{1\ cm\ Hg} \tag{2}$$

82

PRE-LAB QUESTIONS

1. A gas occupies a volume of 15.8 mL at 758 torr and 25°C. What will its volume be if the pressure on it is decreased to 694 torr, and the temperature remains constant?

2. Examine Figure 1. Assume the manometer is filled with water, that $h_1 = 38.6$ cm and $h_2 = 76.5$ cm. If the atmospheric pressure is 742 mm Hg, what is the pressure of the enclosed gas in mm Hg?

SAFETY GOGGLES

1. **APPARATUS ASSEMBLY.** Assemble the apparatus as shown in Figure 1. Insert the stopper tightly into the flask, and mark the bottom of the flask with a grease pencil. Disconnect the flask, fill it with water to the grease pencil mark and carefully pour the water into a graduated cylinder to determine the flask volume. Record the volume on the data table as the **flask volume**. With the flask still disconnected, raise the leveling bulb until the water reaches the top of the buret. Then, lower the bulb until the water reaches the buret bottom. To make sure that no air bubbles remain in the connecting hose, repeat this procedure several times. Raise or lower the bulb so that the water is near the middle of the buret and then tightly insert the stopper into the flask.

2. **LEAK TEST.** Raise the leveling bulb far above the water level in the buret and keep it there. Observe the level of the water in the buret. If it remains in one position after two or three minutes, there are no leaks and the apparatus is ready to be used. Note that at this point you have trapped a fixed quantity (and number of moles) of gas, the volume of which is the flask volume plus the buret volume plus a negligibly small volume in the connecting hose.

3. **MEASUREMENTS.** The gas pressure is altered by raising or lowering the bulb as explained in the introduction. For each measurement, record:

   (a) the volume of gas in the buret, to the nearest 0.1 mL,

   (b) the distance from the bench-top to the water in the buret, h_1, to the nearest 0.1 cm and

   (c) the distance from the bench-top to the water in the leveling bulb, h_2, also to the nearest 0.1 cm. Remember, the meter stick is used to measure distances, and when the bulb is below the bench-top, the distance L is negative.

   Perform five trials:

   1. Leveling bulb and buret water levels the same.

   2. Bulb raised the maximum distance above the buret.

   3. Bulb approximately half-way between trials 1 and 2.

   4. Bulb lowered the maximum distance below the buret.

   5. Bulb approximately half-way between trials 1 and 4.

4. CALCULATIONS. As shown in the data table, calculate the total gas volume (V_{total}), total gas pressure (P_{total}), and product of total volume and gas pressure (Boyle's Law constant) for each of the five trials.

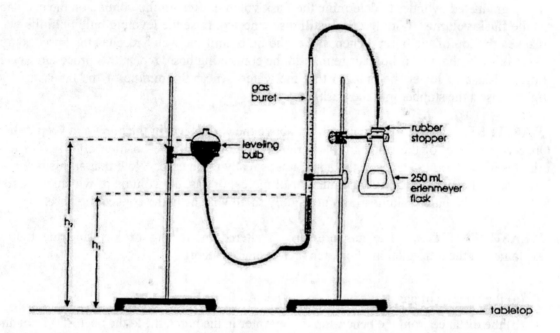

Figure 1. Boyle's Law Apparatus

Student Name_____ Partner's Name(s)_____

Date_____ Course/Section_____ Instructor_____

EXPERIMENT # 7
BOYLE'S LAW
LABORATORY REPORT

Show any calculations in the spaces provided..

DATA AND CALCULATIONS

1.	Densities	1.00 g/mL H_2O		13.59 g/mL Hg		
2.	Flask volume	_____ mL				
3.	Barometric pressure (from instructor)	_____ mm Hg = _____ cm Hg = _____ cm H_2O				

Volume readings

Buret volume	_____	_____	_____	_____	_____	mL
Flask volume	_____	_____	_____	_____	_____	mL
Total gas volume	_____	_____	_____	_____	_____	mL

Height measurements (meter stick)

Leveling bulb (h_2)	_____	_____	_____	_____	_____	cm H_2O
Buret (h_1)	_____	_____	_____	_____	_____	cm H_2O
Difference ($h_2 - h_1$)	_____	_____	_____	_____	_____	cm H_2O

Pressures

$P_{total}=P_{bar} +(h_2 - h_1)$	_____	_____	_____	_____	_____	cm H_2O

Boyle's Law Constant (cm H_2O x mL)

P_{total} x V_{total}	_____	_____	_____	_____	_____	$\times 10^5$

POST-LAB QUESTIONS

1. Calculate the average value of the Boyle's Law constant you determined in today's experiment.

   (b) How many significant figures does your average value of the Boyle's Law constant have?

   (c) Based upon the number of significant figures in your average value for the Boyle's Law constant, what range of values do the rules of significant figures indicate?

   (d) Is the product of pressure × volume constant within the limits of experimental error for your five trials? Hint: Are all of your values within the range predicted in part c?

3. Do your results validate Boyle's Law? Answer yes or no and explain.

4. Make a graph of volume vs. pressure for your data. What is the shape of this graph?

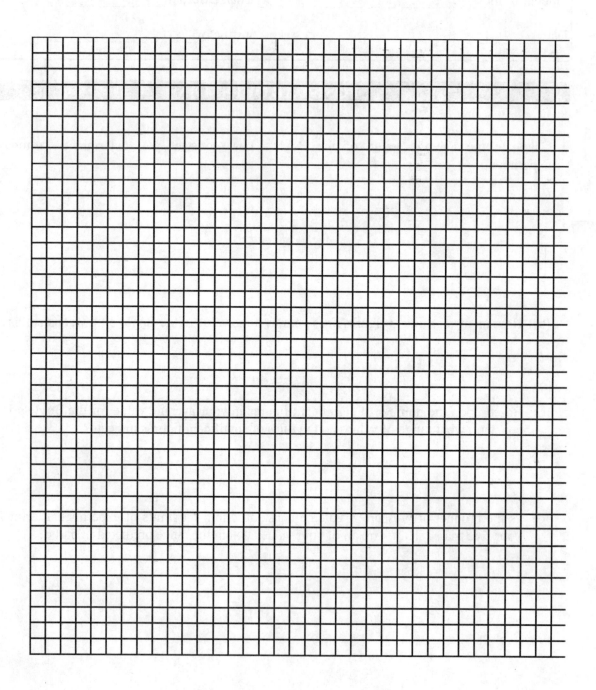

EXPERIMENT # 8
PERCENT OF POTASSIUM CHLORATE IN A MIXTURE

To determine the percentage of potassium chlorate ($KClO_3$) in a mixture of potassium chlorate and potassium chloride (KCl).

INTRODUCTION

When heated, potassium chlorate decomposes into potassium chloride and oxygen gas. The reaction is catalyzed by the presence of manganese dioxide (MnO_2). The equation for the decomposition is:

$$2KClO_3\,(s) \rightarrow 2KCl\,(s) + 3O_2\,(g) \tag{1}$$

From the equation, it is apparent that for every three moles of oxygen gas produced, two moles of potassium chlorate are decomposed. In this reaction, the oxygen is given off into the atmosphere and the resulting loss of mass of the reaction mixture is equal to the mass of oxygen produced. We can calculate the mass of potassium chlorate used by the following:

First, we calculate the moles of oxygen gas produced:

$$\text{mol } O_2 = \text{grams } O_2 \times \frac{1 \text{ mol } O_2}{(\text{GFM } O_2) \text{ grams}} \tag{2}$$

Then, we calculate the number of moles $KClO_3$ consumed using the stoichiometry of the balanced equation:

$$\text{mol } KClO_3 = \text{mol } O_2 \times \frac{2 \text{ mol } KClO_3}{3 \text{ mol } O_2} \tag{3}$$

Finally, we calculate the number of grams of $KClO_3$:

$$\text{grams } KClO_3 = \text{mol } KClO_3 \times \frac{(\text{GFM } KClO_3) \text{ grams}}{1 \text{ mol } KClO_3} \tag{4}$$

The percentage of KClO$_3$ in the original mixture is the mass of potassium chlorate divided by the mass of the original mixture times 100.

$$\%KClO_3 = \frac{mass\ KClO_3}{mass\ of\ the\ mixture} \times 100\%$$ (5)

The potassium chloride in the original mixture is unaffected by the heating process.

PRE-LAB ASSIGNMENT

1. A mixture of KCl and $KClO_3$ has a mass of 2.565 grams. The mixture is heated and the $KClO_3$ is decomposed. After cooling, its mass is found to be 1.987 grams. Perform each of the following calculations and show all work.

   (a) Calculate the mass of oxygen lost from the mixture.

   (b) Calculate the number of moles of O_2 lost from the mixture.

   (c) Calculate the number of moles of $KClO_3$ in the original mixture.

   (d) Calculate the mass of $KClO_3$ in the original mixture.

   (e) Calculate the percentage of $KClO_3$ in the original mixture

Obtain from the cart a numbered unknown container and record the unknown number on the data page. Open the container and visually inspect the sample to confirm that it appears uniform throughout with no clumps. If there are clumps break them up by tightly closing the container and shaking it. If the lumps are still present then use a clean spatula to break them up.

Place a small beaker on the balance, and tare the balance to zero. Place a clean dry test tube (150mm) in the beaker and record its mass to the nearest 0.001 gram. Introduce *approximately* 2.5 grams of the unknown into the test tube. Record the mass of the test tube and unknown mixture.

Holding the test tube in a nearly horizontal position gently shake it to spread out the unknown so that the sample is distributed approximately halfway up the side of the tube. Clamp the test tube in a nearly horizontal position, as shown in Figure 1. Keep it pointed away from other people. Heat

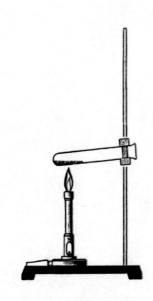

Figure 1. Heating Apparatus for decomposition of $KClO_3$.

the sample, gently at first using the outer cone of the flame, by slowly moving the Bunsen burner back and forth along the length of the tube. When the sample appears translucent throughout, begin to strongly heat the sample by focusing the inner cone of the flame on the lower portion of the test tube so that the tube begins to glow red. Continue this heating process moving up the tube until the entire sample has been intensely heated. Check for completeness of reaction by placing a glowing wooden splint at the mouth of the test tube. If it re-ignites or glows more strongly, continue the heating process described above for an additional five minutes. Continue testing for completeness of reaction and re-heating if necessary until the reaction has reached completion. Allow the test tube to cool to room temperature, and record its mass.

Calculate the mass of oxygen, the moles of oxygen, the moles of potassium chlorate, the grams of potassium chlorate and the percentage of potassium chlorate in the original mixture.

Repeat the procedure with a fresh sample of the same unknown, and average your results on the data table.

96

Student Name_____ Partner's Name(s)_____

Date_____ Course/Section_____ Instructor_____

EXPERIMENT # 8
PERCENT OF POTASSIUM CHLORATE IN A MIXTURE
LABORATORY REPORT

Show any calculations in the spaces provided. Be sure to write your unknown # below.

DATA AND CALCULATIONS

UNKNOWN #_____

TRIAL # 1

Calculations

1. Mass of empty test tube _____g

2. Mass of empty test tube _____g
   + mixture

3. Mass of test tube + residue _____g
   (after heating)

4. Mass of mixture _____g

5. Mass of oxygen _____g

6. Moles of oxygen _____mol

7. Moles of $KClO_3$ _____mol

8. Mass of $KClO_3$ _____g

9. Percent $KClO_3$ in mixture _____%
   (by mass)

Calculations

1. Mass of empty test tube   _____g

2. Mass of empty test tube   _____g
         + mixture

3. Mass of test tube + residue   _____g
         (after heating)

4. Mass of mixture   _____g

5. Mass of oxygen   _____g

6. Moles of oxygen   _____mol

7. Moles of $KClO_3$ _____mol

8. Mass of $KClO_3$ _____g

9. Percent $KClO_3$ in mixture   _____%
         (by mass)

In the spaces provided below calculate the average percentage of Trial 1 and Trial 2. Show work.

Average percent $KClO_3$ _____%

POST-LAB QUESTIONS

1. How would your value for the percent of $KClO_3$ be affected by each of the following errors? Explain your reasoning.

   (a) The test tube is not heated long enough to decompose all of the $KClO_3$.

   (b) After weighing, some mixture spills out as you assemble the apparatus.

   (c) The test tube used has some moisture in it when you begin the experiment.

EXPERIMENT # 9

THE EMPIRICAL FORMULA
OF A CHLORIDE OF MAGNESIUM

PURPOSE

To prepare a compound of magnesium and chlorine, determine its empirical formula and determine the percent of magnesium.

INTRODUCTION

In this experiment, magnesium will be reacted to form magnesium chloride, a binary compound.

In this experiment, a known mass of magnesium metal (Mg) will be converted into soluble magnesium chloride by reaction with hydrochloric acid (HCl). The other product, hydrogen (H_2), escapes the solution as a gas. Excess hydrochloric acid and water are removed by evaporation, leaving pure magnesium chloride.

$$Mg_{(s)} + HCl_{(aq)} \rightarrow Mg_xCl_{y(aq)} \tag{1}$$

$$Mg_xCl_{y(aq)} + heat \rightarrow Mg_xCl_{y(s)} \tag{2}$$

The increase in mass of the sample represents the mass of chlorine that combined with the magnesium. The magnesium-chlorine mass ratio identified allows us to calculate the empirical formula of the compound.

The empirical formula of a compound is the simplest whole number ratio of the two elements. For example, if a compound is found to contain 0.623 moles of potassium for every 0.312 moles of oxygen atoms the formula for the compound would be $K_{0.623}O_{0.312}$ which can be simplified by dividing each subscript by the smaller of these numbers, 0.312, to yield $K_{1.996}O_1$ or K_2O as the empirical formula.

Based upon the fixed charges of magnesium and chloride ions, the theoretical empirical formula can be determined. From this theoretical empirical formula the theoretical percentage of each element can be determined. For instance, the empirical formula of calcium chloride is determined to be $CaCl_2$. From this empirical formula the percentage of calcium is calculated as the mass of calcium percentage in the mass of calcium chloride compound.

102

PRE-LAB QUESTIONS

1. A 0.632 gram sample of a metal, M, (atomic mass = 154.2) is converted into its chloride by dissolving in HCl. 0.923 grams of metal chloride were produced.

    (a) Calculate the percentage of metal, by mass, in the compound.

    (b) What is the empirical formula for the metal chloride?

EXPERIMENTAL PROCEDURE

READ the entire procedure BEFORE you begin the experiment.

> **NOTE: Verify with your instructor that the fume hoods are functioning properly prior to conducting the experiment.**
>
> **Conduct the entire experiment in the fume hood!**

1. A clean dry 150 mL beaker will be used as the **reaction vessel.** The white "marking area" should be clean to permit identification of your experiment. Paper labels MUST BE REMOVED. Electric hot plates (heat setting #3.5) are set up for your use in the fume hood area.

2. Clean the beaker and dry it with a paper towel. Use a pencil to mark it with your initials. Warm the beaker on a hot plate for two to three minutes. Then, place the beaker on the bench top next to the hotplate and allow it to cool. Weigh the beaker, recording its mass to a precision of 0.001 grams.

3. Obtain a sample of magnesium metal (as a 10 cm piece of ribbon) from the laboratory cart. Hold the ribbon with a small piece of paper towel to prevent transfer of moisture and body oils from your skin. Using scissors from the laboratory cart cut the ribbon into eight to ten equally-sized pieces, and transfer them into the dry, weighed beaker. Weigh the beaker and contents, and record the mass to a precision of 0.001 grams.

4. Verify that the magnesium sample is approximately 0.100 to 0.150 grams. Consult your instructor if it is not.

5. Add approximately 10 mL of distilled water (use your 10 mL graduated cylinder), and then add approximately 30 drops of 9.0 M hydrochloric acid (HCl). Effervescence (bubbles) will be observed as the gaseous hydrogen escapes the solution. GENTLY swirl the container to mix the contents.

   IF effervescence (bubbling) stops and magnesium metal is still present, add another 10 to 12 drops of 9.0 M HCl.

IF a WHITE CRYSTALLINE SOLID is observed in the beaker, the magnesium chloride solution is saturated and excess solid has come out of solution. Add an additional four to five mL of distilled water to dissolve the solid.

Continue to gently mix the contents until effervescence (bubbles) ceases.

The dissolving process is complete when the solution is clear and no solids are observed in the bottom of the beaker.

4. Put the beaker on a hot plate (heat setting 3.5) in the hood (escaping HCl gas is irritating) and allow the liquid to evaporate. DO NOT permit the solution to boil vigorously; solids will be lost.

5. After the contents appear dry, continue heating the beaker for an additional four to five minutes. Then move the beaker (caution – HOT!) to the bench top next to the hot plate and allow it to cool. Weigh the beaker and its contents and record the mass to a precision of 0.001 grams.

6. Reheat the beaker and its contents for three to four minutes, allow it to cool, and reweigh. Continue this heating-cooling-weighing process until two successive masses agree within 0.005 grams (constant mass has been achieved). Use the smaller of these two masses in your calculation.

 DISPOSAL of product: Wash the magnesium chloride residue into the sink drain with flowing tap water.

7. After you have recorded the final mass, dissolve the magnesium chloride in tap water. Rinse the resulting solution down the laboratory sink with flowing tap water.

Student Name_____ Partner's Name(s)_____

Date_____ Course/Section_____ Instructor_____

EXPERIMENT # 9
EMPIRICAL FORMULA
LABORATORY REPORT

DATA

		Trial 1	Trial 2
1.	Mass of dry beaker	_____ g	_____ g
2.	Mass of beaker + magnesium	_____ g	_____ g
3.	Mass of beaker + magnesium chloride (initial heating)	_____ g	_____ g
4.	Mass of beaker + magnesium chloride (final heating)	_____ g	_____ g

CALCULATIONS

		Trial 1	Trial 2
1.	Mass of magnesium chloride	_____ g	_____ g
2.	Mass of magnesium	_____ g	_____ g
3.	Mass of chlorine	_____ g	_____ g
4.	Moles of magnesium atoms	_____ mol	_____ mol
5.	Moles of chlorine atoms	_____ mol	_____ mol
6.	Empirical formula of the compound	_____	_____
7.	Theoretical % of magnesium (*Periodic Table*)	_____ %	_____ %
8.	Experimental % of magnesium from data	_____ %	_____ %
9.	Percent error	_____ %	_____ %

POST-LAB QUESTIONS

1. Explain how each of the following experimental errors would affect the value for the percentage of magnesium calculated in this experiment.

   (a) The sample was not dried completely at the end of the experiment.

   (b) A small piece of magnesium was lost after the weighing, but before the reaction was performed.

EXPERIMENT # 10
MOLECULAR MASS OF A VOLATILE LIQUID

To calculate the molecular mass of a volatile liquid by measuring the mass, volume, pressure, and temperature of its vapor and utilizing the ideal gas equation.

In this experiment, we make use of the ideal gas equation:

$$PV = nRT \tag{1}$$

where P is the pressure, V is the volume, n is the number of moles, T is the Kelvin temperature and R is the universal gas constant. The value of R is 0.08206 L-atm/mol-K. The units given with R dictate the units that must be used in this equation. This equation, which is for an ideal gas, holds quite nicely for real gases under the conditions of this experiment.

A small sample of a volatile liquid is introduced into the flask and the flask assembly is placed in a hot water bath as shown in Figure 1. At the beginning of the experiment, the flask is filled with air plus this small amount of liquid. While in the hot water bath, the liquid boils and produces vapor, which forces the air out of the flask through the pinhole in the foil cap. When the liquid appears to be gone, the flask now contains vapor only. Its temperature is the temperature of the water in the bath; its volume is the volume of the flask and its pressure is atmospheric pressure.

At this point, the flask is cooled and the air, which had been displaced, returns into the flask so that the increase in mass is the mass of what had been vapor. We calculate the number of moles of vapor (n) by rearranging Equation 1:

$$n = \frac{PV}{RT} \tag{2}$$

We then calculate the molecular mass, M, by dividing the mass of vapor, g, by the number of moles, n:

$$M = \frac{g}{n} \tag{3}$$

PRE-LAB ASSIGNMENT

1. A sample of an unknown liquid is vaporized in a 255-mL flask in a hot water bath at 100.0° C. The atmospheric pressure is 748 torr and the vapor is found to have a mass of 0.714 grams. What is the molecular mass of the vapor?

2. A gas is found to be 85.7% carbon and 14.3 % hydrogen by mass. Its molecular mass was found to be 98.1 g/mol using the method of this experiment. What is the molecular formula of this gas?

Obtain a DRY 250-mL Erlenmeyer flask and remove any paper labels from it. The flask will be sitting in hot water and any labels would soak off, changing the weight. Take this flask, an aluminum square, and a rubber band over to the lab balances. Without assembling it, weigh the combination. Record this value on the data table. Add about 3 mL of the unknown liquid to the flask, attach the aluminum foil cover and rubber band tightly and make a pinhole in the cover. Be sure this hole is small and that no pieces of tin foil are lost.

Clamp the flask and assemble the apparatus as shown in Figure 1. Adjust the flask and water level so that the flask is immersed as deeply as possible in the hot water bath. Add several boiling chips to the bath to keep the water from "bumping" as it boils. Heat the water to boiling, making note of when the liquid in the flask appears to have completely boiled away. Continue to heat the flask for an additional three minutes after the liquid is completely vaporized. Measure the temperature of the water in the bath, making sure that the thermometer does not touch the beaker.

At this point, release the clamp from the ring stand, and cool the flask under running cold water for about one minute. Do not allow any water to get on the aluminum cap. Carefully and thoroughly dry the flask and its cap, especially under the edge of the foil, but do not open the cap. Weigh the flask, cap and rubber band. The increase in mass is the mass of condensed vapor. Remove the cover and rubber band and discard them. Discard the condensed liquid into the waste bottle provided.

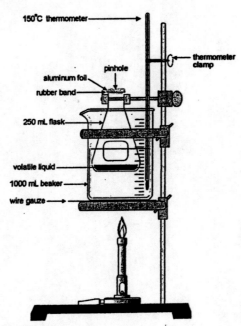

Figure 1. Heating Apparatus for the volatile liquid

Note: Do not let the thermometer stand unattended in the water bath. Hold the thermometer at mid depth while measuring the temperature. Remember to return the thermometer to the protective case when the experiment is complete.

Fill the flask to the very top with water and pour the water into a 500-mL graduated cylinder to obtain the volume of the flask. Record the barometric pressure reading provided by your instructor. This is the gas pressure. The bath temperature is the gas temperature. Calculate the number of moles of vapor using Equation 2, and the molecular mass using Equation 3. Repeat the procedure using different clean dry flask.

EXPERIMENT # 10
MOLECULAR MASS OF A VOLATILE LIQUID
LABORATORY REPORT

DATA

UNKNOWN #____

		Trial 1	Trial 2
1.	Mass of flask + cover	_____ g	_____ g
2.	Mass of flask + cover + condensed vapor	_____ g	_____ g
3.	Flask volume	_____ mL	_____ mL
4.	Barometric pressure	_____ mm Hg	_____ mm Hg
5.	Temperature of boiling water bath	_____ ° C	_____ ° C

CALCULATIONS

		Trial 1	Trial 2
1.	Pressure of vapor (P)	_____ atm	_____ atm
2.	Volume of vapor (V)	_____ L	_____ L
3.	Temperature of vapor (T)	_____ K	_____ K
4.	Mass of vapor (g)	_____ g	_____ g
5.	Moles unknown (n)	_____ mol	_____ mol
6.	Molecular mass (M)	_____ g/mol	_____ g/mol

Calculations

POST-LAB QUESTIONS

1. How would each of the following experimental errors affect the value obtained for the molecular mass? Give your reasoning in each case.

   (a) All of the liquid was not vaporized when the flask was removed from the hot water bath.

   (b) The flask was not dried thoroughly before weighing it at the end of the experiment.

   (c) The flask was left in the hot water bath for an additional thirty minutes after the liquid was completely vaporized.

   (d) The flask was not cooled after removal from the hot water bath.

EXPERIMENT # 11

CALORIMETRY AND SPECIFIC HEAT

PURPOSE

To measure the specific heat of a metal, and to use the results of this to estimate the metal's atomic weight, using the law of Dulong and Petit.

INTRODUCTION

Heat is a form of energy, often referred to as thermal energy, which flows from an object at a higher temperature to one at a lower temperature when the two objects come in contact with one another. The two objects will, after a short time, reach a state of thermal equilibrium, where they are at the same final temperature. If the system is well-insulated, the heat lost by the hotter object will equal the heat gained by the cooler one, a result of the law of conservation of energy. This is the basis for the calculation of the unknown metal's specific heat.

The heat involved in a temperature change depends on three factors: the mass (m) of the object, the temperature change (ΔT) the object undergoes and the specific heat (s) of the substance changing temperature. Specific heat is defined as the heat needed to raise the temperature one gram of the substance by one Celsius degree. Its units, therefore, can be expressed as J/g-C°. Water has a specific heat of 4.184 J/g-C°, Heat, q, (in Joules) is calculated by the equation:

$$q = ms\Delta T \tag{1}$$

Since the metal's specific heat is not known, we cannot calculate q for it, but we can calculate the heat gained by the water. Assuming no heat loss to or gain by the surroundings, we can say that *q (gained by the water) = q (lost by the metal)*.

$$q_m = m_m s_m \Delta T_m \tag{2}$$

$$q_w = m_w s_w \Delta T_w \tag{3}$$

where the subscripts refer to the metal, m and water, w.

Finally, a historically important empirical law for estimating the atomic weight of a metal was discovered by Dulong and Petit many years ago. They found that, for many metals the product of the specific heat and the atomic weight is approximately 25. This experimental rule was one of the few tools early chemists had to estimate atomic weights.

$$sA \approx 25 \tag{4}$$

where s is the specific heat in J/g-C° and A is the atomic weight of the metal.

PRE-LAB ASSIGNMENT

1. A 48.23 gram sample of a metal is heated to 100.0 °C and then dropped into 85.4 grams of water originally at 21.3 °C. The mixture reaches an equilibrium temperature of 24.4 °C. Use 4.184 J/g-C° as the specific heat of water.

    (a) How much heat is gained by the cool water?

    (b) How much heat is lost by the hot metal?

    (c) What is the specific heat of the metal?

2. If a metal was found to have a specific heat of 0.127 J/g-°C, based on the law of Dulong and Petit what is the identity of this metal?

Determine the mass of the unknown metal by taring a large empty test tube (standing in a beaker) to zero and adding the metal sample to the clean dry test tube. Assemble the hot water bath as shown in Figure 1. Fill a 400-mL beaker about two-thirds with water and heat it to boiling. Place the test tube containing the metal in a test tube clamp. Attach the test-tube clamp to the ring stand so that the test tube is suspended in the hot water. Be sure that the water level in the beaker is above the metal level in the test tube, and that the test tube does not rest on the bottom of the beaker. Begin heating the water.

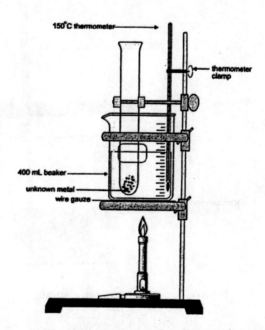

Figure 1. Heating apparatus for the metal sample

While the water bath is being heated obtain the parts of the calorimeter shown in Figure 1. The calorimeter consists of two nesting styrofoam cups with a cover that has a hole for a thermometer. Tare the balance with the styrofoam cups, add about 50 mL of water to it. Record this value on the data table as the *mass of the water*. Measure the temperature of the water to the nearest 0.1°C. Record this value on the data table as the *initial temperature of the water*.

Allow the water bath to boil for at least ten minutes to ensure that the metal is at the same temperature as the boiling water. At this point measure the boiling water bath temperature with a thermometer. Record this value on the data table as the *initial temperature of the metal*.

After recording the temperature of the metal quickly, and in one motion, remove the test tube containing the metal from the boiling water bath and transfer the metal into the styrofoam calorimeter. Avoid allowing any hot water to be added to the cup. Place the cover on the calorimeter, and use the thermometer to gently stir the metal and water. Record to 0.1°C the highest temperature reached by the water. Record this value of the data table as the *equilibrium temperature of the metal and water*.

Dry the metal sample by heating it in the hot water bath in a test tube and then spreading it out on a dry paper towel. Repeat the experiment using a dry test tube and a fresh sample of water. When the experiment has been completed, dry the sample again, and return it in the test tube from which it originally came.

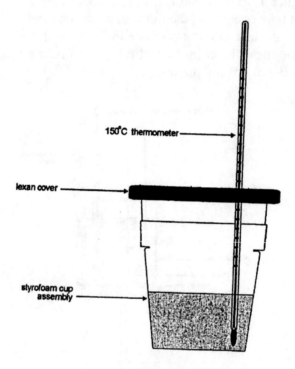

150°C thermometer

lexan cover

styrofoam cup assembly

Figure 2. Styrofoam calorimeter

Student Name_____ Partner's Name(s)_____

Date_____ Course/Section_____ Instructor_____

EXPERIMENT # 11
CALORIMETRY AND SPECIFIC HEAT
LABORATORY REPORT

Show any calculations in the spaces provided. Be sure to write your unknown # on your report sheet.

DATA AND CALCULATIONS

UNKNOWN #_____

TRIAL # 1

Calculations

1. Mass of metal   _____g

2. Mass of water   _____g

3. Initial temperature of the metal   _____°C
    (in the boiling water)

4. Initial temperature of the water
    (before the addition of the metal)   _____°C

5. Equilibrium (final) temperature of   _____°C
    the metal and water

6. q for the water   _____J

7. q for the metal   _____J

8. Specific heat of the metal   _____J/g-C°

9. Approximate atomic weight   _____g/mol

10. Identity of the metal   _____

DATA AND CALCULATIONS

TRIAL # 2

Calculations

1. Mass of metal _____ g

2. Mass of water _____ g

3. Initial temperature of the metal _____ °C
   (in the boiling water)

4. Initial temperature of the water
   (before the addition of the metal) _____ °C

5. Equilibrium (final) temperature of _____ °C
   the metal and water

6. q for the water _____ J

7. q for the metal _____ J

8. Specific heat of the metal _____ J/g-C°

9. Approximate atomic weight _____ g/mol

10. Identity of the metal _____

POST - LAB QUESTIONS

1. The specific heat of aluminum is 0.90 J/g-C°. How much heat must be added to a 245-gram aluminum pot containing 556 grams of water to raise the temperature from 22.1°C to 97.4°C? What percentage of this heat is used to heat the aluminum pot?

2. For each of the following experimental errors clearly state if the error would increase, decrease, or have no effect on the specific heat that you determined in today's experiment. You *must* explain your reasoning.

   (a) A small piece of metal was lost after its mass was determined, but before it was heated.

   (b) The metal sample was removed from the boiling water bath, but was not immediately transferred to the calorimeter.

EXPERIMENT # 12

CONDUCTIVITY, BONDING AND IONIC REACTIONS

To study some properties of ionic and covalent compounds; to test the electrical conductivities of compounds and their aqueous ions; to study a few acid-base ionic reactions.

INTRODUCTION

Ionic and Covalent Bonds.

Atoms bond with other atoms in order to obtain a more stable electronic structure. When active metals combine with active non-metals, they generally do so by a transfer of electrons from the metal to the non-metal. The resulting particles (atoms that have gained or lost electrons) are called ions, and the attraction these oppositely charged ions have for each other constitutes an ionic bond. An example of this would be the reaction of sodium with chlorine.

$$Na^{.} + \overset{..}{\underset{..}{Cl}}: \longrightarrow Na^{+} + :\overset{..}{\underset{..}{Cl}}:^{-} \tag{1}$$

At room temperature ionic compounds are generally hard crystalline solids in which the crystal lattice is an arrangement of alternating positive and negative ions. When these ions are freed from the lattice by melting (fusion) or dissolving in water, they become excellent conductors of electricity. Substances whose aqueous solutions conduct electricity are called **electrolytes**. Solid ionic compounds do not conduct electricity because the ions are not mobile.

Covalent bonds result when two atoms share one or more pairs of electrons to complete their outer shells. For instance, the formation of H_2 or HCl from individual atoms of hydrogen and chlorine:

$$H^{.} + .H \longrightarrow H:H \tag{2}$$

$$H^{.} + \overset{..}{\underset{..}{Cl}}: \longrightarrow H:\overset{..}{\underset{..}{Cl}}: \tag{3}$$

In the formation of H_2, the electrons are shared equally, and the symmetrical distribution of charge results in a **non-polar covalent bond**. The formation of HCl results in an unequal sharing of electrons because chlorine is a much more electronegative element than hydrogen. This makes the H-Cl bond more positive at the hydrogen end of the bond and more negative at the chlorine end of the bond. We say the H-Cl bond is a **polar covalent bond**. The particles formed as a result of covalent bonding are called molecules. When covalent substances form solids, these individual molecules occupy the lattice points in the crystal. Examples of covalent molecular substances are sugar, $C_{12}H_{22}O_{11}$, wax and plastics.

Most covalent molecular substances are not electrolytes. Acids are the exception to this rule. Acids are molecular compounds that are electrolytes. This is due to the fact that when they dissolve in water, like ionic compounds, they form ions. **Strong acids**, such as hydrochloric acid (HCl), break up into ions completely, resulting in every HCl molecule forming one H^+ and one Cl^- ion.

$$HCl\,(g) \;\rightarrow\; H^+\,(aq) \,+\, Cl^-\,(aq) \tag{4}$$

When **weak acids** dissolve in water only some of the molecules break up into ions. For instance, when acetic acid ($HC_2H_3O_2$) dissolves in water only a small fraction of the molecules ionize to form H^+ and $C_2H_3O_2^-$ ions.

Strong acids are said to be **strong electrolytes** because they conduct electricity very well when dissolved in water. This reflects that every molecule of a strong acid ionizes when dissolved. Weak acids are said to be **weak electrolytes** because they ionize only to a small extent, and their solutions are poor conductors compared to strong acids.

Ionic compounds must dissociate into ions in order to dissolve. Therefore, soluble ionic compounds form solutions that conduct electricity well. Soluble ionic compounds are therefore also considered strong electrolytes.

The hydrogen ion H^+ has no electrons and therefore bonds that are formed to it must come from other atoms. Bases are substances that have a lone pair of electrons that can be used to form a bond to other substances such as H^+. The most common base used in the chemistry laboratory is the hydroxide ion, OH^-. When hydroxide ion reacts with H^+ the reaction below occurs. This is called a **neutralization reaction**.

$$H^+\,(aq) + OH^-\,(aq) \;\rightarrow\; H_2O\,(l) \tag{5}$$

Ionic Reactions

The ionic reactions studied in this experiment are reactions between acids and bases. A typical reaction would be that of nitric acid with sodium hydroxide. The equations below show, respectively, the balanced **molecular equation**, the **complete ionic equation** and the **net ionic equation** for the reaction.

$$HNO_3\,(aq) \;+ NaOH\,(aq) \;\rightarrow\; NaNO_3\,(aq) + H_2O\,(l) \tag{6}$$

$$H^+\,(aq) + \; NO_3^-\,(aq) + Na^+\,(aq) + OH^-\,(aq) \;\rightarrow\; Na^+\,(aq) + NO_3^-\,(aq) + H_2O\,(l) \tag{7}$$

$$H^+\,(aq) + OH^-\,(aq) \;\rightarrow\; H_2O\,(l) \tag{8}$$

In order to provide a complete description of a reaction in solution a description of the state of each of the substances should be included. If a pure substance is present it is designated solid, liquid or gas using (s), (l), or (g). If a substance is soluble it will be dissolved and is designated as aqueous (aq). The solubility rules for ionic compounds may be referred to when writing chemical equations for reactions in solution. The solvent itself, water in this case is always designated (l) as if it was a pure liquid substance. To obtain the total ionic equation from the molecular equation all the strong electrolytes (soluble ionic compounds and strong acids) are written as individual dissolved ions (aq). Weak electrolytes and all other molecular compounds are not written as individual ions–they appear in the same state as they did in the molecular equation. To obtain the net ionic equation from the total ionic equation the spectator ions (all the species that appear in the same state on both sides of the reaction) are crossed out. The new equation obtained is the net ionic equation. The net ionic equation is the briefest description of a reaction in solution.

Ionic reactions occur whenever ions are removed from solution by means of a reaction. This occurs when water forms, an insoluble substance precipitates, gas forms. The formation of water was shown above; an example of precipitate formation is the reaction of solutions of $AgNO_3$ with NaCl:

$$Ag^+ (aq) + NO_3^- (aq) + Na^+ (aq) + Cl^- (aq) \rightarrow AgCl (s) + Na^+(aq) + NO_3^- (aq) \qquad (9)$$

These reactions result in the removal of ions from solution and lead to a decrease in conductivity.

Some reactions may form ions and result in an increase in conductivity. An example would be:

$$NH_3(aq) + HC_2H_3O_2(aq) \rightarrow NH_4^+ (aq) + C_2H_3O_2^- (aq) \qquad (10)$$

If the same ions are present in solution before and after reaction, then no reaction has occurred, as in the mixing of aqueous NaCl and KBr.

$$Na^+ (aq) + Cl^- (aq) + K^+ (aq) + Br^- (aq) \rightarrow Na^+ (aq) + Cl^- (aq) + K^+ (aq) + Br^- (aq) \quad (11)$$

The net ionic equation for this reaction would have no overall change occurring.

In Part 1, of this experiment you will measure the conductivity of solids and liquids/solids dissolved in water to determine whether the substances are electrolytes or non-electrolytes. In Part 2, of this experiment you will measure the conductivity of reaction mixtures to determine the effect of chemical reactions on the number of ions present.

PRE-LAB ASSIGNMENT

1. The following compounds are nearly insoluble in water: $AgCl$, $CaCO_3$, $BaSO_4$ and $ZnCO_3$. All alkali metal compounds and all nitrates are soluble in water. Write ionic equations and net ionic equations of the following reactions. If no reaction occurs, write **No Reaction**.

    (a) $LiCl$ (aq) + $AgNO_3$(aq) $\rightarrow$

    (b) $NaNO_3$ (aq) + KI (aq) $\rightarrow$

    (c) KOH (aq) + H_2SO_4 (aq) $\rightarrow$

    (d) $BaCl_2$ (aq) + Na_2SO_4 (aq) $\rightarrow$

The Conductivity Apparatus. The apparatus, as shown in Figure 1, consists of a pair of solid brass probes connected to a simple, battery-powered state-of-the-art electronics circuit. The display contains ten discrete multi-colored LEDs and twenty levels of measurement using the high and low display settings. When a conductor is introduced between the two electrodes, the circuit is complete and the LEDs will cascade to a final reading. The "HIGH" circuit allows measurement of greater conductivities than the "LOW" circuit. The higher the number of the LED reading, the greater the conductivity of the sample. LED Dx "HIGH" readings that are between **10** and **6** are generally good conductors. LED Dx "HIGH" readings that are between **5** and **0** are generally poor conductors. All readings from the LED Dx "LOW" circuit imply very low conductivities and are very poor or non-conductors.

INSTRUCTIONS for RCI–Dx Conductivity Meter

Place the solid or liquid to be tested into an individual   well of the   spot plate (see Figure 2). Immerse the electrodes of the conductivity meter into the well. Depress the "HIGH" button waiting to see if any LEDs light. If some LEDs light wait until cascading stops and record the numerical LED reading indicating which scale (HIGH or LOW) on your data table. If you are unable to achieve a LED reading, indicate a NR (No Reading) on your data table.

• Use no more than twenty drops of a test solution in a spot plate so that the metal electrodes will make proper contact.

• Rinse the spot plate and electrodes with distilled water between every trial. When testing solids, dry the electrodes as well as possible with paper towels.

• To restore the electrode surface to a new-like state use very fine steel wool to polish the electrodes.

Figure 1. RCI-Dx Conductivity Meter

1. Electrolytes and non-electrolytes.
(a) Use the conductivity apparatus to explore the nature of a number of substances and their aqueous solutions. A list of substances and their solutions is included on your report sheet.

(b) Compare the relative strengths of 0.1 M hydrochloric acid (HCl) and 0.1 M acetic acid ($HC_2H_3O_2$) by performing the following reactions:

    i. Use forceps to place a single piece of a marble chip in each of two wells on a spot plate and add about 20 drops of each acid to each well.

    ii. Use forceps to place a tiny piece of zinc into each of two wells on a spot plate and add about 20 drops of each acid to these.

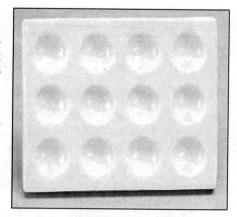

Figure 2. Spot plate

Report on the relative strength of these acids by observing the rates at which CO_2 and H_2 gases are generated from the marble chips and zinc, respectively.

2. Typical ionic reactions.

For each reaction, we will try to determine the nature of the products by observing the conductivity of the individual reactants and the resulting products. We are observing whether the conductivity increases, decreases or remains unchanged, and interpreting this in the context of ions consumed or produced. For each reaction, write an ionic equation. Then, write the net ionic equation.

(a) 0.1M HCl with 0.1M NaOH. Test the conductivity of each 0.1M solution, then mix equal volumes together and test one-half of the resulting solution.

(b) 0.1M $HC_2H_3O_2$ with 0.1M NH_3. (The NH_3 solution may be labeled as NH_4OH). Test equal volumes of the separate solutions, mix them and retest the conductivity.

(c) 0.1M H_2SO_4 with 0.1M $Ba(OH)_2$. Test the separate solutions. Then, while the electrodes are in the H_2SO_4 solution, add one drop of phenolphthalein solution and begin adding the $Ba(OH)_2$ solution to it while stirring. As you approach the endpoint of the reaction, add the $Ba(OH)_2$, drop-by-drop, until the last drop added causes a permanent pink color. Note the changes in conductivity as you add $Ba(OH)_2$ and the conductivity of the final mixture. Observe the formation of a precipitate.

After each experimental test, pour the contents of your spot plate into a 150 mL beaker at your workstation. Wash the spot plate thoroughly with copious amounts of water at the laboratory sink and dry it thoroughly. When you have completed all experimental tests pour the contents of your waste beaker into the waste container provided by your instructor.

Student Name_____ Partner's Name(s)_____

Date_____ Course/Section_____ Instructor_____

EXPERIMENT # 12
CONDUCTIVITY, BONDING AND IONIC REACTIONS
LABORATORY REPORT

PART 1A ELECTROLYTES AND NON-ELECTROLYTES

- *Record the LED reading from your conductivity apparatus.*
- *List the Relative Conductivity of each substance and solution tested (good, poor or non-conductor).*
- *Identify the Type(s) of particle(s) present (ions, molecules or both).*

Sample	LED Reading	Relative Conductivity	Type(s) of Particle(s)
H_2O (distilled)			
H_2O (tap)			
NaCl (s)			
0.1M NaCl (aq)			
C_2H_5OH (l)			
C_2H_5OH (aq)			
0.1 M $HC_2H_3O_2$ (aq)			
$C_{12}H_{22}O_{11}$ (s)			
$C_{12}H_{22}O_{11}$ (aq)			

PART 1B   ELECTROLYTES AND NON-ELECTROLYTES

- *Record the LED reading from your conductivity apparatus.*
- *Describe the rates of the reaction of the two acids with marble chips and with zinc:*

Sample	HCl		HC$_2$H$_3$O$_2$	
	LED Reading		LED Reading	
Marble chips	Results		Results	

Sample	HCl		HC$_2$H$_3$O$_2$	
	LED Reading		LED Reading	
Zinc	Results		Results	

Student Name_____   Course/Section_____

Date_____   Instructor_____

PART 2   TYPICAL IONIC REACTIONS

- *Record the LED Reading from your conductivity apparatus.*
- *List the Relative Conductivity of each solution tested (good, poor or non-conductor).*

a. Reactants before mixing

	LED Reading	Relative Conductivity		LED Reading	Relative Conductivity
0.01 M HCl			0.01 M NaOH		

a. Reaction mixture

	LED Reading	Relative Conductivity
0.01 M HCl + 0.01 M NaOH		

b. Reactants before mixing

	LED Reading	Relative Conductivity		LED Reading	Relative Conductivity
0.1 M $HC_2H_3O_2$			0.1 M NH_3		

b. Reaction mixture

	LED Reading	Relative Conductivity
0.1 M $HC_2H_3O_2$ + 0.1 M NH_3		

c. Reactants before mixing

	LED Reading	Relative Conductivity		LED Reading	Relative Conductivity
0.1 M H_2SO_4			0.1 M $Ba(OH)_2$		

c. Reaction mixture

	LED Reading	Relative Conductivity
0.1 M H_2SO_4 + 0.1 M $Ba(OH)_2$		

POST - LAB QUESTIONS

1. Based on your observations of the rate of the reactions in Part 1a, which acid is stronger? Explain why.

2. Write the complete ionic equations for the three reactions performed in Part 2 of the experiment.

3. Write the net ionic equations for the three reactions performed in Part 2 of the experiment.

4. Based upon net ionic equation from Part 2c of the experiment, explain the pattern in your conductivity data before and after mixing the reactants.

EXPERIMENT # 13
BUILDING MOLECULAR MODELS
FROM LEWIS STRUCTURES

PURPOSE

a) To practice drawing Lewis Structures for molecules and polyatomic ions.
b) To construct models of these molecules/ions in order to explore their structure, shape, polarity and chemical reactivity.

INTRODUCTION

Read the sections of your textbook on drawing Lewis structures and VSEPR theory. Familiarize yourself with the octet rule.

Lewis Structures

A Lewis Structure is a visual representation of the valence electron configuration of a molecule or polyatomic ion. The rules for drawing a Lewis structure are based upon the patterns that chemists have observed in molecules and polyatomic ions that are known to be stable. Therefore, they are useful in predicting the stability of substances that are not yet known to exist.

The vast majority of stable substances are found to have Lewis structures that obey the **octet rule**. The octet rule states that substances tend to form molecules or ions where each atom has a total of eight electrons directly surrounding them either in bonding pairs or non-bonding (lone) pairs. When counting electrons for the octet rule, bonding electrons are counted as part of the octet for *each* atom involved in the bond. Hydrogen is an exception to the octet rule. Hydrogen is most stable with two electrons, making a single bond. This is referred to as the duet rule – it *only* applies to hydrogen. The duet rule tells us that hydrogen is never found in between atoms because if it had two bonds it would exceed the duet rule.

The octet rule is most strictly obeyed by the elements carbon, nitrogen, oxygen, and fluorine. In the rare cases where these four elements do violate the octet rule they are always found to have *less* than an octet These four elements have *never* been observed to have more than an octet. While these four elements represent only a small fraction of the periodic table, they comprise many important compounds, including the majority of those that are essential for life. These elements also comprise the majority of substances considered in the area of organic chemistry. Elements beyond the third row (below C, N, O and F) on the periodic table *usually* follow the octet rule. However, for elements in this portion of the periodic table it is possible to violate the octet rule by having more or less than an octet – a topic not discussed here.

Skeletal Structures

The first step in the process of drawing a Lewis structure is forming a hypothesis about how the atoms are connected together. This is known as the **skeletal structure** of the substance. For molecules and polyatomic ions that have a small number of atoms there may be only one *possible* skeletal structure. For instance, silane (SiH_4) has the Lewis structure shown below.

Silane

$$H$$
$$\overset{\displaystyle H}{\underset{\displaystyle H}{H-Si-}}$$

This structure is *the only* possible way to connect these atoms together *and* obey the duet /octet rules. The hydrogen atoms can only have one bond so they must all surround the single silicon atom.

Isomers

For some chemical formulas there is more than one possible way to draw the skeletal structure. For instance the four atoms in the chemical formula HOCN can be arranged with the two different skeletal structures shown below. Both of these structures obey the octet rule!

$$H-\ddot{O}=C=\ddot{N}$$
Cyanic acid

$$H-\ddot{N}=C=\ddot{O}$$
Isocyanic acid

Each of these skeletal structures is a different **isomer** of the chemical formula HOCN. Each structure represents a different substance with different physical and chemical properties. When a scientist determines the chemical formula of an unknown substance sometimes more than one skeletal structure can be drawn. If this is the case then all the possible Lewis structures that obey the duet/octet rules for each isomer are considered. Further experiments are then performed to determine which of the possible skeletal structures correctly describes the physical and chemical properties of the isomer they have discovered.

Resonance Structures

For a given skeletal structure there are sometimes several ways to distribute the electrons creating structures where all the atoms obey the duet/octet rule. These structures are known as **resonance structures**. For instance, the three structures below all have the same chemical formula, the same skeletal structure, and all have octets on all the atoms.

Sulfur Dioxide $\left[\begin{array}{ccc} \ddot{O} = \ddot{S} - \ddot{O} \colon & \longleftrightarrow & \colon \ddot{O} - \ddot{S} = \ddot{O} \end{array}\right]$

| Resonance structures are drawn in square brackets with double-ended arrows, as shown for sulfur dioxide |

These two structures are not isomers since they have the same skeletal structure. Substances that have resonance structures are often more stable than substances that do not have them. The properties of the molecule or polyatomic ion are usually found to reflect an *average* of the different possible resonance structures. For sulfur dioxide (SO_2) the strength of both of the S-O bonds is found to be identical, and is in between the strength typically observed for a single and a double bond.

Isoelectronic Structures

Elements that are in the same group of the periodic table were originally grouped together by Mendeleev based upon the similarity of the chemical reactions they underwent. Modern chemists believe this similarity is the result of elements in the same group possessing the same number of **valence electrons**. Molecules or polyatomic ions that share the same skeletal structure *and* have the same number of total valence electrons are said to be **isoelectronic**. Isoelectronic substances are often found to bear strong chemical similarity to each other, just like elements of the same group on the periodic table. For instance, carbon monoxide (CO) and cyanide ion (CN^-) both have ten valence electrons and identical skeletal structures (just two connected atoms). They are isoelectronic.

$\colon C \equiv O \colon$ 　　　　　 $\colon C \equiv N \colon^-$

Carbon Monoxide 　　　　　 Cyanide ion

Despite the fact that carbon monoxide is a molecular substance that exists as a gas at room temperature, and that cyanide is an ion they share some chemical properties. For instance, both are extremely toxic poisons.

Predictive Power of Lewis Structures

If a Lewis structure that obeys the octet rule can be drawn for an unknown molecule or polyatomic ion, the substance is probably stable enough to exist. If a Lewis structure that obeys the octet rule *cannot* be drawn for a molecule or polyatomic ion, this indicates that the substance is probably unstable. This does not necessarily mean this substance does not ever exist, but it does indicate that if it does exist it will probably be unstable and therefore very reactive. Many such substances are of critical importance in chemical reactions. Due to their instability they may only exist briefly before decomposing into stable products. For unstable substances the Lewis structure that *that comes as close as possible* to obeying the octet rule is often useful in predicting their chemical properties. For instance, the ion shown below is an example of a carbocation (a positive ion formed from an organic compound). It is formed as an intermediate in some chemical reactions.

Tertiary Butyl Cation

Notice that the structure above does not have an octet on the central carbon atom. The structure does come as close as possible to obeying the octet rule – *most* of the carbon atoms have octets and the hydrogen atoms all have duets. This structure is useful in predicting the chemical reactivity of this ion. This ion very readily becomes involved in chemical reactions that introduce one more bonding pair to the carbon atom to achieve an octet as in the reaction shown below.

Radicals

Substances that have an odd number of valence electrons are called **radicals**. Radicals *cannot* obey the octet rule. To draw the best possible Lewis structures for a radical follow the steps for creating a Lewis structure until you have a substance with one electron *more* than the substance actually has. To obtain the correct structure simply remove a single electron from any lone pair in the structure. If more than one atom has a lone pair to provide this electron then removing the electron from each of these atoms creates a different resonance structure. An example of such a substance is the molecule nitrogen oxide (NO) which has 11 valence electrons. Two resonance structures for nitrogen oxide, *neither of which* obeys the octet rule, are shown below.

Nitrogen Oxide

Rules for Drawing Lewis Structures

1. Calculate the total the number of valence electrons in the molecule or polyatomic ion.
   - Use the Periodic Table to the number of valence electrons for each atom. For main group elements the number of valence electrons is the Roman Numeral group number.
   - Add up the valence electrons of each atom in the molecule or polyatomic ion.
   - For anions, add electrons (equal to the negative charge) to the total number of valence electrons. For cations, subtract electrons (equal to the positive charge) from the total number of valence electrons.

2. Draw the skeletal structure for the molecule/polyatomic ion.
   - In the skeletal structure all the atoms are connected by single bonds. More bonds may be added later.
   - Hydrogen atoms can only form one bond so they cannot be in between atoms.
   - Sometimes more than one skeletal structure can be drawn. Each one is a different isomer of that molecule or polyatomic ion.

3. Give octets to all atoms in the skeletal structure (except hydrogen) by placing lone pairs on them.

4. Count the total number of valence electrons in this structure.

5. If the Lewis structure contains the correct number of valence electrons it is complete and has no resonance structures that obey the octet rule.

6. If the structure contains more valence electrons than the molecule or polyatomic ion has then reduce the number of valence electrons in the structure by erasing lone pairs on adjacent atoms and replacing them with a bonding pair between those atoms.

   - Each bond that replaces two adjacent lone pairs reduces the valence electron count by two.
   - The maximum number of bonds that may be placed between main group elements is three – a triple bond.
   - If there are no adjacent atoms with lone pairs then a Lewis structure that obeys the octet rule does not exist. Removing lone pairs to correct the valence electron count will create possible structures that have less than an octet on some atoms.
   - If there is more than one way to remove the necessary number of valence electrons creating double or triple bonds then each of the resulting structures is a different resonance structure.
   - If the molecule or polyatomic ion is a radical then lower the valence electron count to one more than the Lewis structure should contain as described above. Finally, remove a single electron from a lone pair to correct the valence electron count. If there is more than one atom that this electron can be taken from then each of the resulting Lewis structures is a different resonance structure.
   - If the structure contains fewer valence electrons than the molecule or polyatomic ion has then add the necessary number of valence electrons to the structure by placing lone pairs on atoms that are capable of having expanded octets.

VSEPR Theory

The geometric arrangement of atoms around a single atom they are all bonded to is referred to as the molecular geometry around that atom. For molecules or polyatomic ions with a single central atom the geometry around that atom is used to describe the shape of the entire molecule. This is referred to as the molecular shape of the molecule or polyatomic ion itself. The theory that is used to predict molecular shape is known as: Valence Shell Electron Pair Repulsion (VSEPR) theory.

The concept of VSEPR theory is that the groups of valence electrons in the bonding regions between atoms and the lone pairs of atoms form groups that repel each other. The repulsion is due to all of the VSEPR groups having the same negative charge since they all consist of electrons. The VSEPR groups arrange themselves around the central atom to make their bond angles as large as possible, in order to minimize the repulsion between them.

The following VSEPR table indicates the molecular shape around an atom of interest, (the atom shaded grey in each sketch) based on the number of VSEPR groups attached to that atom. The VSEPR groups are shown as either bonded atoms (unshaded circles) or lone pairs (shaded balloons). **Note that atoms attached by single or double and triple bonds, lone pairs, and unpaired electrons in radicals each count as one VSEPR group.**

So for instance, hydrogen sulfide (H_2S) has four VSEPR groups on the central carbon atom. Two of these are lone pairs and two are bonding pairs.

$$\text{Hydrogen Sulfide} \quad H\!-\!\overset{\bullet\bullet}{\underset{\bullet\bullet}{S}}\!-\!H$$

The VSEPR table below indicates that the molecular shape of hydrogen sulfide is bent.

The molecular shape indicated in the table below describes the geometry around *any* atom with the number of lone and bonding pairs indicated in the sketch, regardless of whether or not that atom is the central atom of the molecule. For instance, the molecule ethane, C_2H_6, does not have a single central atom.

$$\text{Ethane} \quad H\!-\!\overset{\displaystyle H \quad H}{\underset{\displaystyle H \quad H}{C\!-\!C}}\!-\!H$$

The molecular geometry around both carbon atoms can be said to be tetrahedral since each carbon atom has four bonding groups attached (see last entry in the VSEPR table below). However, this is not an accurate description of the molecular shape of the ethane molecule. Describing the shape of molecules or polyatomic ions that do not have a single central atom is an advanced topic not addressed in this exercise.

Note: Several molecular geometries that are not encountered in this exercise have been omitted from the table below.

Molecular Shape	Sketch	Description
Linear (AX₂ & AX)	or	Two atoms around a central atom which has no lone pairs results in a linear geometry. The bond angles are 180°. Any two atoms connected together are in a linear geometry, but there is no bond angle since there are only two atoms.
Trigonal Planar (AX₃)		Three outer atoms surround the central atom. There are no lone pairs on the central atom. The central and outer atoms all lie in the same plane (molecule is flat). Bond angles are exactly 120°.
Bent (AX₂E)		Two outer atoms and one lone pair surround the central atom. Bond angles are slightly less than 120°.
Tetrahedral (AX₄)		Four outer atoms surround the central atom. There are no lone pairs on the central atom. The four outer atoms are evenly arranged in 3D around the central atom as if at the corners of a regular tetrahedron. The bond angles are exactly 109.5°.
Trigonal Pyramidial (AX₃E)		Three outer atoms and one lone pair surround the central atom. Here the central atom is located slightly above the three outer atoms, like a tripod. The bond angle is slightly less than 109.5°.
Bent (AX₂E₂)		Two outer atoms and two lone pairs surround the central atom. Bond angles are slightly less than 109.5°.

Electronegativity and Bond Polarity

Some atoms in molecules have the ability to pull shared electrons closer to themselves than other atoms, an ability referred to as electronegativity. **Electronegativity** (χ) is a periodic property that generally increases going across a period and decreases going down a group. Some selected electronegativity values are shown below in Table 1.

Atom	Electronegativity
Fluorine	4.0
Oxygen	3.5
Nitrogen	3.0
Carbon	2.5
Boron	2.0
Hydrogen	2.1
Chlorine	3.0
Sulfur	2.5
Phosphorous	2.1
Iodine	2.5

Table 1. Electronegativities of selected elements

If two bonded atoms have different electronegativities, then the bond pair electrons will be shared unequally between them. The atom with the greater electronegativity will pull the bond electrons closer towards itself, causing it to obtain a partial negative charge (δ-). The atom with the lower electronegativity will have bond electrons pulled further away from it, causing it to obtain an equal positive charge (δ+). If the difference in electronegativities between the two atoms is larger than 0.40 the result is a **polar covalent bond.** If two bonded atoms have a difference between their electronegativities that is less than or equal to 0.40, then the bonding electrons will be shared equally or almost equally. The result is a **non-polar covalent bond.**

Molecular Polarity

Molecular polarity results when the entire molecule (not just a bond in the molecule) ends up with an unequal distribution of electrons. In general, a molecule will be **polar** if it contains polar bonds that are distributed in a non-symmetrical arrangement around the central atom. A non-symmetrical arrangement typically results when there are lone pairs on the central atom or when different outer atoms surround the central atom.

Not surprisingly, a molecule will be **non-polar** if it contains all non-polar bonds. A molecule will also be non-polar if it contains polar bonds distributed in a symmetrical arrangement around the central atom. The symmetry causes the individual bond polarities to cancel out, resulting in a net non-polar molecule. A symmetrical arrangement typically results when there are no lone pairs on the central atom and if all the outer atoms are identical.

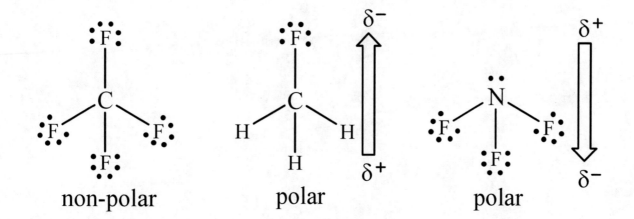

non-polar   polar   polar

PRE-LAB ASSIGNMENT

1. For each of the molecules or polyatomic ions in the data table of this experiment calculate the total number of valence electrons. Show your calculation on the data table in pencil so that it may be corrected before building the model.

2. Draw Lewis structures for each of the molecules and polyatomic ions on the data table of this experiment. For parts 1-6, if more than one resonance structure that obeys the octet rule is possible then draw any *one* of these structures. Draw all of the structures in pencil so that they may be corrected before building the model. Clearly show all bond pair electrons as lines and lone pair electrons as pairs of dots or a single line.

Constructing Models

Guidelines for Constructing Molecular Models

1. Each colored ball in your kit corresponds to a different atom. Refer to the list below to select the correct colored ball for each type of atom.

Ball Color	Number of holes	Atom Type	Number in the kit
Black	4	C	4
White	1*	H	12
Blue	4	N	3
Green	4	B or Cl	6
Green	3**	B	1
Purple	4	I or P	2
Red	4	O	9
Yellow	4	S	2

   * This ball has only one hole since H obeys the duet rule.

   ** Since this ball has only three holes it is used to represent an atom that has a sextet (6 electrons) not an octet

2. The ball selected must have the same number of holes in it as the atom has bonding pairs + lone pairs + single non-bonding electrons.
3. Use the **short grey sticks** for single bonds. There should be **13** in your kit.
4. Use the **long flexible grey sticks** for double or triple bonds. There should be **16** in your kit. To create the bonds insert the sticks into holes on each of the balls. It will be necessary to bend the sticks in order to create double or triple bonds.
5. Use the **flat beige balloon shaped pieces** for representing the position of lone pairs of electrons. There should be **42** in your kit.
6. Use a **short purple stick** for representing a single non-bonding electron. There should be **2** in your kit.

After you have constructed the models for each part of the experiment have your instructor verify that they are built correctly and initial the data page before answering the question on the data table.

Part 1: Construct the models for N_2, O_2 and NO^-. Have your instructor verify that the models have been built correctly. Determine whether each molecule is polar or non-polar, its bond angles, and its molecular shape. Record this information on the data table. Before taking apart these models answer Question 1 on the data table.

Part 2: Construct the models for CCl_4, CH_2Cl_2 and CH_4 Have your instructor verify that the models have been built correctly. Determine whether each molecule is polar or non-polar, its bond angles, and its molecular shape. Record this information on the data table. Before taking apart these models answer Question 2 on the data table.

Part 3: Construct the models for NH_3, BH_3, and NH_3BH_3. Have your instructor verify that the models have been built correctly. Determine whether NH_3 and BH_3 are polar or non-polar, their bond angles, and molecular shapes. Record this information on the data table. Before taking apart these models answer Question 4 on the data table.

Part 4: Construct the models for CO_2, CS_2, OCN^- and N_2O. Have your instructor verify that the models have been built correctly. Determine whether each molecule is polar or non-polar, its bond angles, and its molecular shape. Record this information on the data table. Before taking apart these models answer Question 5 on the data table.

Part 5: Construct the models for BO_3^{3-}, CO_3^{2-}, and NO_3^-. Have your instructor verify that the models have been built correctly. Determine whether each molecule is polar or non-polar, its bond angles, and its molecular shape. Record this information on the data table. Before taking apart this model answer Question 6 on the data table.

Part 6: Construct the models for Cl, Cl^-, and IO_2. Use a purple single bond connector to represent a single electron in a radical. Have your instructor verify that the models have been built correctly. Determine whether each molecule is polar or non-polar, its bond angles, and its molecular shape. Record this information on the data table. Before taking apart these three models answer Question 7 on the data table. Based upon your answer to question 7 construct the model for $IO_2^?$. Determine it is polar or non-polar, its bond angles, and its molecular shape. Record this information on the data table.

Part 7: Construct the models for all the resonance structures of NCCN, $H_2C_3H_2$, PO_2^{3-}, and NO_2^-. Have your instructor verify that the models have been built correctly. Determine whether each molecule is polar or non-polar, its bond angles, and its molecular shape. Record this information on the data table. Before taking apart these models answer Question 8 on the data table.

Student Name_____ Partner's Name(s)_____

Date_____ Course/Section_____ Instructor_____

EXPERIMENT # 13
BUILDING MOLECULAR MODELS FROM LEWIS STRUCTURES
LABORATORY REPORT

Molecule	Total Valence Electrons	Lewis Structure	Polarity Bond Angles Molecular Shape	
N_2			Polar ☐ Non-Polar ☐	
			Molecular Shape	
O_2			Polar ☐ Non-Polar ☐	
			Molecular Shape	
NO^-			Polar ☐ Non-Polar ☐	
			Molecular Shape	

Question #1 Based on your examination of the models you have built which of these three contains the shortest chemical bond?

Instructor Approval
of the Models above_____

Molecule	Total Valence Electrons	Lewis Structure	Polarity Bond Angles Molecular Shape	
CCl_4			Polar ❐ Non-Polar ❐	
			Bond Angle	
			Molecular Shape	
		Skeletal structure has C as the central atom		
CH_2Cl_2			Polar ❐ Non-Polar ❐	
			Bond Angle	
			Molecular Shape	
		Skeletal structure has C as the central atom		
CH_4			Polar ❐ Non-Polar ❐	
			Bond Angle	
			Molecular Shape	
		Skeletal structure has C as the central atom		

Question #2 Based on the polarity of each of these molecules which would you predict to be the most soluble in water? Hint: recall the "like dissolves like" rule from an earlier lab experiment.

Instructor Approval
of the Models above_____

Molecule	Total Valence Electrons	Lewis Structure	Polarity Bond Angles Molecular Shape	
NH₃			Polar ☐ Non-Polar ☐	
			Bond Angle	
			Molecular Shape	
BH₃			Polar ☐ Non-Polar ☐	
			Bond Angle	
			Molecular Shape	
NH₃BH₃				

Question #3 Examine the models you have built for the three substances in the reaction below

$$BH_3 + NH_3 \rightarrow BH_3NH_3$$

Based upon your models, which atom do the electrons come from that forms the B-N bond in BH_3NH_3?

Instructor Approval
of the Models above_____

Molecule	Total Valence Electrons	Lewis Structure	Polarity Bond Angles Molecular Shape	
CO_2		Skeletal structure has C as the central atom	Polar ❑ Non-Polar ❑	
			Bond Angle	
			Molecular Shape	
CS_2		Skeletal structure has C as the central atom	Polar ❑ Non-Polar ❑	
			Bond Angle	
			Molecular Shape	
OCN^-		Skeletal structure has C as the central atom	Polar ❑ Non-Polar ❑	
			Bond Angle	
			Molecular Shape	
N_2O		Skeletal structure has a N as the central atom	Polar ❑ Non-Polar ❑	
			Bond Angle	
			Molecular Shape	

Question #4 Which of the above substances are isoelectronic with each other?

Instructor Approval
of the Models above_____

Molecule	Total Valence Electrons	Lewis Structure	Polarity Bond Angles Molecular Shape	
BO_3^{3-}			Polar ☐ Non-Polar ☐	
			Bond Angle	
		Skeletal structure has B as the central atom	Molecular Shape	
CO_3^{2-}			Polar ☐ Non-Polar ☐	
			Bond Angle	
		Skeletal structure has C as the central atom	Molecular Shape	
NO_3^{-}			Polar ☐ Non-Polar ☐	
			Bond Angle	
		Skeletal structure has N as the central atom	Molecular Shape	

Question #5 Examine the pattern in the chemical formulas and charges of the three isoelectronic ions above. Based on this pattern what is the chemical formula and charge of the next member of this series?

Instructor Approval
of the Models above_____

Molecule	Total Valence Electrons	Lewis Structure	Polarity Bond Angles Molecular Shape		
Cl			Polar ☐ Non-Polar ☐		
			Bond Angle		
			Molecular Shape		
Cl^-			Polar ☐ Non-Polar ☐		
			Bond Angle		
			Molecular Shape		
IO_2			Polar ☐ Non-Polar ☐		
			Bond Angle		
			Molecular Shape		
		Skeletal structure has I as the central atom			
$IO_2^?$			Polar ☐ Non-Polar ☐		
			Bond Angle		
			Molecular Shape		
		Skeletal structure has I as the central atom			

Question #6 The charge of many ions can be predicted by drawing the Lewis structure of the uncharged substance of the same chemical formula and determining how many electrons would have to be added or removed to achieve an octet on all atoms. For instance, the Lewis structure of a chlorine atom does not have an octet since chlorine has only seven valence electrons. The addition of one electron forms the chloride ion that obeys the octet rule and has charge of -1. Based upon examination of the model you have built for IO_2 predict the charge on the ion with the chemical formula $IO_2^?$ and record its polarity, bond angles and molecular shape above.

Instructor Approval
of the Models above_____

Molecule	Total Valence Electrons	Lewis Structure
NCCN		Skeletal structure has the atoms in the order N-C-C-N
$CH_3CO_2^-$		Skeletal structure has a C-C bond, no O-H bonds and both O's are on the same C
PO_2^{3-}		Skeletal structure has P as the central atom
NO_2^-		Skeletal structure has a N as the central atom

Question #7 For each of the substances above draw the Lewis structures and build the models for all the possible resonance structures. Are any of these substances isoelectronic?

Instructor Approval
of the Models above_____

EXPERIMENT # 14
WATER OF HYDRATION

To study some properties of hydrated salts; to determine the percentage of water and the formula of a hydrated compound.

A hydrated salt is one in which some definite number of water molecules is attached to each formula unit of the salt. Generally, these waters of hydration are bonded to the positive ions of the salt. A typical example of a hydrate is copper (II) sulfate pentahydrate, $CuSO_4 \bullet 5\ H_2O$, in which five water molecules are attached to each $CuSO_4$. When a hydrate is heated strongly, the waters of hydration are driven off and the remaining anhydrous salt is left behind:

$$CuSO_4 \bullet 5H_2O \quad \rightarrow \quad CuSO_4 + H_2O \qquad (1)$$

hydrated salt anhydrous salt

Sometimes the color of the salt changes as it is dehydrated, and the crystals change their appearance as well. The mass of the water in the hydrate can be calculated by determining the mass lost as a result of heating. The percentage of water in the original hydrate can then be calculated from the equation below.

$$\% H_2O \quad = \quad \frac{mass\ of\ water}{mass\ of\ hydrate} \times 100 \qquad (2)$$

For example, in $BaCl_2 \bullet n\ H_2O$ the value of n can be calculated by converting the mass of water lost during heating into moles of water, and the mass of the anhydrous salt ($BaCl_2$) remaining after heating into moles of $BaCl_2$. The number of moles in each formula unit of the hydrated salt (n) can then be calculated as the ratio of moles of water lost to moles of anhydrous $BaCl_2$ that remained.

$$n \quad = \quad \frac{moles\ H_2O}{moles\ anhydrous\ salt} \qquad (3)$$

The value of n is generally an integer.

In some hydrates, the waters of hydration are so loosely bound that the hydrate will lose water to the atmosphere upon standing. This property is known as efflorescence. Other anhydrous ionic compounds tend to absorb water readily from other substances. These are said to be hygroscopic, and they are often used as dessicants or drying agents. Some, like sodium hydroxide, NaOH, absorb so much water that they dissolve in the absorbed water. This process is called deliquescence.

In this experiment we study qualitatively the behavior of some of these substances, and then we quantitatively analyze a hydrate to find the percentage of water in it and its complete formula.

PRE-LAB ASSIGNMENT

1. A sample of hydrated magnesium sulfate, $MgSO_4$, has a mass of 3.645 grams. It is heated to drive off the water until a constant mass of 1.778 grams is finally obtained.

    (a) Calculate the percent by mass of water in the hydrate.

    (b) Calculate the moles of water and the moles of anhydrous $MgSO_4$ in the sample.

    (c) What is the hydrate's complete formula?

SAFETY

GOGGLES

1. Effect of heat and reversibility of dehydration.

(a) Place several crystals of hydrated $CuSO_4$ in a test tube. Hold the test tube in a nearly horizontal position, and heat gently. Record any changes that you observe.

(b) Place several crystals of hydrated $CoCl_2$ in an evaporating dish. Place the evaporating dish on a wire gauze and ring, and heat to dryness. Record any changes that you observe.

(c) After each has cooled, add several drops of water, and observe any color changes. Discard contents of test tubes into the waste container provided.

2. Efflorescence and deliquescence. Place several crystals of $CuSO_4 \bullet 5H_2O$, $Na_2SO_4 \bullet 10H_2O$ and anhydrous $CaCl_2$ on uncovered watch glasses, and allow them to stand until the laboratory period is nearly over. Note any changes. Discard the solids in the waste container provided.

3. Use as a drying agent. Place some anhydrous $CaCl_2$ in the bottom of a test tube. Then, hold the test tube horizontally, and add a few a crystals of $CuSO_4 \bullet 5H_2O$ to the other side. Stopper the tube, and observe the appearance of each at the end of the laboratory period. Discard as before.

4. Percentage of water in a hydrated salt. Heat a clean crucible with its cover strongly for two minutes to dry them thoroughly. After cooling, measure their combined mass to the nearest 0.001 gram and record it on the data table. Also make note of the cover's mass separately in case it should break during the experiment. Add 3-4 grams of the hydrate to the crucible, and weigh the crucible, cover and contents. Heat the crucible with the lid slightly ajar, gently at first, and then more strongly, until the salt changes from a crystalline form to a powder (about fifteen minutes). Allow it to cool with the cover on; then weigh again. Calculate the percentage of water in the hydrate and the hydrate's formula using Equations 2 and 3.

Student Name_____ Partner's Name(s)_____

Date_____ Course/Section_____ Instructor_____

EXPERIMENT # 14
WATER OF HYDRATION
LABORATORY REPORT

OBSERVATIONS

1. Effect of heat and reversibility of dehydration.

	Describe the changes that you observed.	
	when heated	*after addition of water*
$CuSO_4 \bullet 5H_2O$		
$CoCl_2 \bullet 6H_2O$		

2. Efflorescence and deliquescence

	observations	*property*
$CuSO_4 \bullet 5H_2O$		
$Na_2SO_4 \bullet 10H_2O$		
Anhydrous $CaCl_2$		

3. Use as a drying agent.

Describe and explain the changes that occurred in the test tube containing anhydrous CaCl$_2$ and hydrated CuSO$_4$.

DATA AND CALCULATIONS

4. Percentage of water in a hydrate.

UNKNOWN #_____

Show any calculations in the spaces provided. Express all answers to the proper number of significant figures

Calculations

1. Mass of crucible and lid   _____ g

2. Mass of crucible, lid and hydrate   _____ g

3. Mass of crucible, lid and
    anhydrous salt   _____ g

4. Mass of water lost   _____ g

5. Mass of hydrate   _____ g

6. Experimental % water in hydrate   _____ %

7. Theoretical % water (from formula)   _____ %

8. Percent error   _____ %

9. Moles of water produced   _____ mol

10. Moles anhydrous salt   _____ mol

11. Ratio:
    mol H$_2$O/mol anhydrous salt   _____

12. Formula of the hydrate   _____ • ___ H$_2$O

POST-LAB QUESTIONS

1. How would each of the following procedural errors affect the value for the percentage of water obtained? Explain.

   (a) The crucible was not thoroughly dry at the beginning of the experiment.

   (b) The hydrate was not heated long enough.

   (c) The crucible was heated so strongly that the $MgSO_4$ decomposed to form solid MgO and gaseous SO_2.

APPENDIX A

READING A VOLUMETRIC DEVICE

Step 1: Determine the scale increment:

To find the scale increment, subtract the values of any two adjacent labeled graduations and divide by the number of intervals between them.

QUESTION: What is the scale increment for the 10-mL graduated cylinder at the right?

ANSWER: First subtract 8 mL - 6 mL = 2 mL. Next, count that there are ten intervals between the labeled graduations. Therefore, the scale increment is 2 mL/10 graduations = 0.2 mL/graduation.

Step 2: Use the graduations to find all certain digits:

Use the labeled graduations and the scale increment to find the certain digits in the measurement.

QUESTION: What are all of the certain digits for solution in the 10-mL graduated cylinder shown above?

ANSWER: The first digit is 6, since the last labeled graduation below the meniscus is 6. Next, use the scale increment. There are three unlabeled graduations below the meniscus, and each graduation represents 0.2 mL, for an additional 0.4 mL. Therefore, the certain digits of the reading are 6.4 mL.

Step 3: Estimate the uncertain digit and obtain a reading:

Estimate the distance that the meniscus lies between the two graduations as a decimal fraction and multiply by the scale increment.

QUESTION: What is the volume you should record for the solution in the image above?

ANSWER: The meniscus is about four tenths of the way to the next graduation, so the final digit in the reading is (0.4 increment) × (0.2 mL/increment) = 0.08 mL. The uncertain reading is added to the certain digits, so the volume measurement is 6.48 mL.

APPENDIX B
CONVERSION FACTORS

MASS SI unit is the kilogram (kg)	LENGTH SI unit is the meter (m)	VOLUME SI unit is the cubic meter (m^3)
*1 kg = 1000 g 1 kg = 2.2046 lb *1 lb = 16 oz 1 lb = 453.6 g *1 ton = 2000 lb	*1 m = 100 cm *1 m = 1000 mm 1 m = 39.37 in *1 km = 1000 m *1 mi = 5280 ft 1 mi = 1.609 km *1 in = 2.54 cm	*1 liter (L) = 1000 mL *1 L = 0.001 m^3 1 L = 1.057 qt *1 mL = 1 cm^3 *1 qt = 32 oz *1 gal = 4 qt

PRESSURE SI unit is the Pascal (Pa)	TEMPERATURE SI unit is the Kelvin (K)	METRIC PREFIXES
1 atm = 101.3 kPa *1 atm = 760 torr 1 atm = 14.70 lb/in^2 *1 torr = 1 mm Hg	0 K = − 273.15 °C K = °C + 273.15 °C = 5/9 (°F − 32)	pico (p) = 10^{-12} nano (n) = 10^{-9} micro (μ) = 10^{-6} milli (m) = 10^{-3} centi (c) = 10^{-2} deci (d) = 10^{-1} kilo (k) = 10^{3} mega (M) = 10^{6}

* indicates that these quantities are exactly equal by definition